No More Fossils

Forerunners: Ideas First

Short books of thought-in-process scholarship, where intense analysis, questioning, and speculation take the lead

FROM THE UNIVERSITY OF MINNESOTA PRESS

(Continued on page 82)

No More Fossils

Dominic Boyer

University of Minnesota Press

MINNEAPOLIS

LONDON

ISBN 978-1-5179-1636-7 (PB)
ISBN 978-1-4529-7021-9 (Ebook)
ISBN 978-1-4529-7090-5 (Manifold)

Published by the University of Minnesota Press, 2023
111 Third Avenue South, Suite 290
Minneapolis, MN 55401–2520
www.upress.umn.edu

Available as a Manifold edition at manifold.umn.edu

The University of Minnesota is an equal-opportunity educator and employer.

The author gratefully acknowledges the Berggruen Institute and the University of Southern California whose intellectual and financial generosity made this book possible. Writing in the utopian space of the Bradbury Building was endlessly inspirational, as were so many conversations within the community of Berggruen USC Fellows. Many, many thanks to all who helped.

Contents

1. Living with Fossils

FOSSILS LIVE DEEP IN MEMORY. Growing up in Chicago in the 1970s and 1980s, my family lived in what could be charitably called an "urban environment." Even the yard behind our six-flat was paved in concrete. There was no money for distant family vacations so neighboring Indiana became an occasional escape to nature; our getaway destination maybe once a summer was the Indiana Dunes State Park. I have vivid memories of driving in our small, green, ageless Datsun along the Chicago Skyway, windows rolled down because it was hot, but then quickly rolled back up again when we reached the acrid smoke from the steel refineries and paint plants and the sickly smell of the massive trash dump that grew taller each year.

When we cleared Gary, the air improved and the coastal highway became surrounded by forest of oaks, hickories, and cottonwoods. Sand dusted the soil and now and again we'd catch tempting glimpses of sun-sparkled blue water between stands of trees. My first love was the dunes themselves. Dunes are wonders, sympoietic combinations of strong northern winds, ample beachfront, and the sturdy blades and rhizomic roots of the humble beachgrass that captures airborne sand and sculpts it into giant hills and ridges. Climbing to the top of a dune was arduous work, especially for a child raised in the vertically challenged Midwest. But I can remember no greater achievement than summitting a dune and no greater thrill than running headfirst down one. Each step forward felt like flying before gravity sank my feet deep into the vertiginous sandside.

A timid swimmer, I spent my time on the water's edge while my sisters cavorted in the deeper water. I hunted pebbles and shells, looking for marvels. Once in a while, that close attention was rewarded with a fossil: a gift from the Silurian period, 400 million years ago, when what is now Lake Michigan was a shallow saltwater sea teeming with brachiopods, cephalopods, and corals. I learned much later that I also had glaciers to thank. It was they who had scoured the landscape during the last Ice Age and churned those Silurian fossil sediments to the surface.

Finding fossils in the surf is precarious play, a vivid example of the need to be present for a moment in time. As a wave withdraws one has only a few seconds to recognize and make contact with the deep history of the planet before the water returns again, swirling foam and refraction. Tantalizing hints of form emerge and dissolve, perhaps never to reappear. A fossil find always felt to me more like a cosmic blessing and less the due reward of hard work. Bending over, wandering the surf, I recall encountering favosite coral fossils, the occasional small brachiopod shell, and more rarely the impressions of zooid colonies known as lace coral. Though I didn't realize it at the time I also encountered remarkable stones that revealed the invisible lines of stromalite striations when wet. Their aquatic transformation was mysterious and magical: what I learned only later is that these stromalites were once constellations of photosynthesizing cyanobacteria, the origin of all oxygenic life on the planet and also the oldest of all fossils. Cyanobacteria share a claim to fame with Homo sapiens as the only two species to have decisively impacted the lifeworld of every other species with whom they shared the planet.

My most precious find was a large, beautiful cluster of crinoids, looking like a handful of cheerios embedded in gray-black stone. Once upon a time, they would have been crowned with colorful feathery pinnules that filtered plankton from the sea just like today's sea lilies and feather stars. Indeed, crinoids are one of those remarkable evolutionary success stories, so resilient and adaptable that they haven't evolved much in the past 250 million years. Crinoids can live equally well in tidal pools as in deep ocean trenches; they sense movement, light, and food; they move and swim and sway, they provide shelter for smaller fish and shrimp.

Fossils have likely touched all our lives in some small way; my memories are no more than grains of sand when considered in terms of the rich cultural history of fossils. Historian Adrienne Mayor argues that recent archaeological and paleontological findings reinforce theories that exposed fossils inspired the imagination of some mythological creatures.[1] The beak-nosed protoceratops could have offered a model for the Scythian griffin, mammoth skulls may have served as models for the Greek cyclops, and so on. Many have also speculated that Chinese and European dragon myths were inspired by fossils of large aquatic and avian creatures.

We know that fossils, especially inland marine fossils, attracted the attention of naturalists and philosophers for thousands of years. A common mystery mused about by many observers was how shells had found their way to the tops of mountains far from any obvious body of water. Philosophers like Xenophanes (570–478 BCE) and Shen Kuo (1031–1095) contemplated fossil evidence and used it to discern the dynamic character of land- and seascapes. In Shen's case, fossils helped contribute to an insightful theory of climatological change. As such, fossils were an important catalyst of early geology. But they also offered insights into the nature of life and death. The great Persian philosopher Ibn Sīnā (981–1037) was evidently inspired by fossils to theorize a process of mineralization in his remarkable philosophical treatise, *Kitāb al-shifā'* (The Book of Healing), "If what is said concerning the petrifaction of animals and plants is true, the cause of this (phenomenon) is a powerful mineralizing and petrifying virtue which arises in certain stony

---

1. Adrienne Mayor, *The First Fossil Hunters* (Princeton, N.J.: Princeton University Press, 2000).

spots, or emanates suddenly from the earth during earthquakes and subsidences, and petrifies whatever comes into contact with it."[2]

The word "fossil" first appeared in French and English in the mid-sixteenth century, deriving from the Latin *fossilis,* which literally meant dug out of the earth. "Fossil" was a broad concept in its first century or two of existence, referring to anything interesting or valuable with a subterranean past. For example, the book that has as good a claim as any to coining the modern term—the Swiss physician and polymath Conrad Gessner's 1565, *De rerum fossilium* (On fossil objects)—mostly concerned minerals. It was also the first European scientific text to analyze fossil specimens and to compare them explicitly with living organisms. Gessner noted the similarity, for example, between fossil echinoids and living sea urchins. But the title page of the book features engravings of jeweled rings and gems, suggesting that the true lure of things dug out of the earth was the value and beauty they promised. A Sir Thomas Palmer published a book in 1606 praising the virtues of travel for the "better advancement" of European gentlemen, so long as that travel was conducted both honorably and profitably. On the ledger of profits, Palmer advised that travelers pay close attention to countries' commodities and especially "things hid in the veines and wombe of the earth . . . namely, the Mines of mettals and Fossiles whereof there are such sundrie species."[3]

In this way, "fossil" indexed multiple interests of Early Modern Europe. On the one hand, fossils played a key role in an evolving scientific understanding of planetary forces, histories, and life. As historian Martin Rudwick writes, "In the late 17th and early eighteenth centuries, arguments about the interpretation of the various kinds of 'fossils' were almost as intense as those concerned with, say,

2. Ibn Sīnā, "Upon Mountains," in *Kitāb al-shifāʾ* (Cairo, 22 volumes edited by various scholars, 1952–1983).

3. Sir Thomas Palmer, *An Essay of the Meanes how to Make Our Travailes, Into Forraine Countries, the More Profitable and Honourable* (London: Mathew Lownes, 1606), 83–84.

the basic forces of nature, the ultimate structure of matter, or the essential character of life itself."[4] However, on the other hand, fossils captured a growing interest in discovering, unearthing, and exploiting subsurface resources. This latter confluence of meanings—minerals, valued resources, fossils—is what staged the coining of the term "fossil fuel" in the mid-eighteenth century. Literary theorist Karen Pinkus reminds us that the word "fuel" derives from the old French *foaile*, referring to a bundle of firewood. "Fuel, we might say, begins very early, as a form of combustion inextricable from the hearth, one of the most primeval human traces made on the face of the earth . . ."[5] dating back to hunter-gatherer times. "Fossil fuel," on the other hand, was a prototypical modern and industrial concept referring specifically to coal and peat dug out of the earth to be burned in smelting operations and, later, to fuel steam engines.

"Fossil" today maintains a similar dual meaning. On the one hand, we associate the term with paleontological discoveries, especially dinosaurs (another great childhood obsession, by the way). The second meaning denotes fossil fuels, sources of concentrated energy that have brought both great luxury and misery to the world over the past four centuries. What I wish to spotlight in this book is how fossil fuels, and the forms of cultural life associated with them, have come to be *fossilized* in global civilization.

Fossilization has its own curious conceptual history. Ibn Sīnā's theory of a powerful "petrifying virtue" at work in the world belongs to a much longer scientific tradition of trying to comprehend biological processes of formation. One can find embryologies in ancient Egyptian, Indian, and Greek philosophies, debates as to what kind and how many eggs and seeds were necessary to form lives and to give lives form. Aristotle's biology maintained, for example, that a seed holds within itself the telos (end or purpose) of an adult plant;

4. Martin Rudwick, *Earth's Deep History* (Chicago: University of Chicago Press, 2014), 38.

5. Karen Pinkus, *Fuel* (Minneapolis: University of Minnesota Press, 2016), 12.

the seed always contains a premonition of the mature biological form. This teleological understanding of formation evolved over time and expanded to include models for the association of all life forms. It was part of the medieval Christian belief in a "great chain of being," the alchemical reasoning for transubstantiation and the curious preformationist belief, popular in the seventeenth century, that sperms contained miniaturized adult beings known as homunculi. Aristotelian teleology filtered into vitalist philosophy and pre-Darwinian orthogenetic evolutionary models, like Lamarck's, which saw a *pouvoir de la vie* (enabling force of life) driving organisms to inexorably evolve from simplicity toward complexity.

Historical teleology became the signature of arguably the most influential European philosopher of the nineteenth century, G. W. F. Hegel, and the many evolutionary thinkers that came after him. Hegel wove the Aristotelian imagination of seeds and final forms together with a vision of history advancing through a dialectical cycle of formalization and negation. Fossilization was a crucial aspect of Hegel's model of world history. Culture was like a seed that contained within itself the homunculus of an adult form, the state, which concretized a people's spirit and will. Once a people achieved their purpose in the struggle of history, they could be expected to coast along for a while in a fossilized, routinized period Hegel described as "formal duration."[6] Meanwhile, some new people was being born and maturing to negate the achievements of the old world, setting the stage for a new world-historical chapter of conflict and progress. Later Victorian era evolutionists lacked Hegel's nuanced sense of dialectical contingency. Believing they were already securely on the summit of history, the Victorians gave voice to the worldview of late nineteenth-century European empire, which saw a strikingly linear course to human development culminating in modern European civilization. The progress of technology epitomized European modernity, constantly revolutionizing

6. G. W. F. Hegel, *The Philosophy of History* (New York: Dover, 1956), 75.

life through the innovation of new machines for industry, control over the natural world, and for the accumulation of wealth and luxury. Everything and everyone else was a fossil according to late nineteenth-century Europe, a historical leftover to be trampled or swept aside by the juggernaut of European modernity. Not incidentally, this juggernaut depended wholly on fossil fuels for its operation and expansion.

In contrast to nineteenth-century teleology, what is striking about contemporary scientific accounts of fossilization is their emphasis on how rare and conditional fossilization actually is. It is far more common for a living being to die and then rapidly be dissembled for its component parts by its ecological neighbors than it is for its form to persist. Fossils usually require rapid sedimentation followed by high temperature and pressure conditions over a long period of time. Petrified wood, for example, only forms when, to cite one scientific description, "Ancient trees buried in sediments or volcanic ash . . . petrify when silica-rich water circulates through the wood and slowly replaces its cellular structure with jasper, chalcedony and, less commonly, opal."[7] Ancient zooplankton can only become petroleum under a specialized combination of temperature, pressure, and rock formation. At lower temperature and pressure, the plankton will become waxy kerogen or tarry bitumen. But if it's too hot and compressed, they will become natural gas. Then, the surrounding rock must be porous and permeable enough (like sandstone or limestone) for petroleum to stably accumulate. Finally, a more impermeable rock layer above is needed to trap the petroleum in place and to prevent its migration to the surface. Despite all the power oil exerts above ground today, it is actually a geologically precarious creation.

I find it encouraging to consider the fragility and precarity of fossils. If fossilization is the exception rather than the rule in questions

7. Michael Wise, *Encyclopedia of Geology, Second Edition* (London: Elsevier, 2021).

of planetary life and death, then perhaps it's advisable to challenge the long philosophical and historical tradition of thinking about the progress of civilization as an evolution of stable forms from greater simplicity to greater complexity and even perfection. Instead, we should pay more attention to the constancy and contingency of worldly metamorphosis. As philosopher and historian of science Donna Haraway puts it, "Critters—human and not—become with each other, compose and decompose each other, in every scale and register of time and stuff in sympoietic tangling, in ecological evolutionary developmental earthly worlding and unworlding."[8] Form still matters, of course. But it is just an aspect of the tangling of life and death, the whirl of "lifedeath" as I like to think about it. So, form is neither to be revered nor feared. In that spirit, two lessons from thinking about fossils and fossilization guide this book. The first is that fossilization happens for specific contingent reasons that can be reconstructed with care. The second is that even the most imposing fossils are themselves susceptible to transformation, often becoming surprisingly brittle once they are removed from the environments that gave them shape.

A civilization beyond fossil fuels still seems difficult to grasp, in no small part because of how completely fossil fuels have seeped into our cultural imagination, mineralizing visions of the future in the shape of the fossil fueled past. Just like petrified wood, the cultural forms generated by fossil fuels are vivid and beautiful in their own way. But they also represent ancient life forms that, unlike crinoids, are poorly adapted to further duration on earth. The abundance of petrofossils is now choking out the life possibilities not just of humans but of the vast majority of species on the planet. It is more and more obvious that this fossil-fueled civilization has no sustainable future. It perpetuates an ecological Ponzi scheme stealing away the lives of countless species and the well-being of

8. Donna Haraway, *Staying with the Trouble* (Durham, N.C.: Duke University Press, 2016), 97.

future generations in exchange for contemporary human conveniences (shared unequally even among humans!). Petrofossils need to decompose and dissolve. And ditto many of the carbofossils and sucrofossils that belong to the same petrified tree of history. This book tells the story of the rise of fossil-fueled civilization, explores what continues to stick us in its ooze, and explains what will release us from the quicksand of its past. Another reassuring thing I learned in the course of researching this book is that you can't really drown in quicksand like in the old Hollywood films—liberation is slow, but escape from the remains of the past is not only possible, it is often enough the course of things.

That's of little comfort when one is stuck deep, however. So let's begin wriggling ourselves free. We'll first look backward at the origins of the current ooze. We need to understand its composition if we wish to free ourselves. In the ebb and flow, the surf and sand of history, we are going to become fossil hunters.

2. Sucro, Carbo, Petro, or What Made This World That Needs to Be Remade

I WANTED TO WRITE THIS SHORT BOOK because I've long wondered about the "fossil" in "fossil fuels." What historical relations and actions are ambered in today's petroculture? Could more clarity about what fossilizes us today open paths toward better futures? It turns out we are petrified in many ways. The concept "fossil fuel," as noted above, is a child of European modernity. And, talk about sympoietic tangling, fossil fuels have in turn enabled pretty much everything we consider to be European and modern. But beginning our story with fossilized plants is a bit of an overshoot since they have provided energy and heat to human cultures for a very long time and, for the most part, in ecologically unproblematic ways. In China, for example, surface coal mining dates back at least 5,500 years. That means we'll probably never know exactly how long humans have been making use of coal, tar, and peat to warm hearths and light ways. Quite possibly for as long as they have used firewood. Interestingly, the same can be said of many energy forms glossed as "renewable" today. How long have humans used the sun to warm themselves? Forever. How long have they sought to harness wind and water? Who knows. No one can tell us exactly where and when the sailboat was invented. It was probably invented in many different places on separate timelines.

How fossilized plants became fossil fuels has very little to do with fossils themselves and much more to do with the *fossilization* of sugar politics (what I'll call "sucropolitics" from now on) within European colonial civilization. Those sucropolitics were a decisive accelerant for European modernity in the sixteenth, seventeenth, and eighteenth centuries and their legacies are now mineralized in the ecocidal trajectory of global capitalism. Our story begins with sugarcane (*Saccharum officinarum*).

Humans and sugarcane share an ancient tangle. *Saccharum officinarum* was first domesticated in New Guinea around 8000 BCE and then spread through several waves of diffusion across much of Asia in the millennia that followed. The army of the first great European colonist, Alexander of Macedon, is reputed to have encountered sugarcane in the Indus River valley. They gave it the name *saccharon* meaning a reed that could "bring forth honey without the help of bees."[1] Persia and India pioneered the making of sugar from sugarcane in the centuries before Islamic and Christian empires spread across the world. Though pleasing for its sucrose, sugar was an exotic curiosity. When Europeans encountered it in the centuries that followed, sugar was more often medicinal than culinary, and where culinary it was a precious spice rather than a staple. In his marvelous book, *Sweetness and Power*, anthropologist and historian Sidney Mintz writes that "Sucrose was practically unknown in northern Europe before perhaps AD 1000, and only barely known for another century or two."[2] Southern Europe had a different timeline of encounter because the Arab conquest of North Africa and Spain also brought sugarcane cultivation and sugar production to the Mediterranean from Morocco to Sicily. The Crusades put northern Europeans into sustained contact with sugar-making for the first time; religious warriors and opportunistic merchants

1. Noël Deerr, *The History of Sugar, 2 vols.* (London: Chapman and Hall, 1949), 1:63.

2. Sidney Mintz, *Sweetness and Power* (London: Penguin, 1985), 23.

discovered that sugar was a very lucrative commercial venture. Northern European port cities like Antwerp, Bristol, and Bordeaux established refineries for improving Mediterranean sugar as early as the thirteenth century. Even the plagues that killed half the population of Europe in the fourteenth century indirectly benefited sugar makers by driving up the commodity's price due to labor shortages.

The table was laid out for a European sugar boom in the fifteenth century. In Iberia, where Islamic technological and economic influence had predominated for several centuries, Portugal and Spain became the leading edge of an expanding and modernizing sugar industry. The Iberians used new ship designs like the caravel to island hop from the Mediterranean out into the Atlantic, seeding new sugar ventures wherever they could along the way. The Iberians eventually migrated sugarcane as far south as São Tomé off the coast of West Africa. Founded in 1493, São Tomé became the model for the sugar plantation that the Iberians would spread westward across the Atlantic to the Caribbean and Brazil over the next century. "In terms of plantation size, the universality of slave labor, and production techniques, [São Tomé] was the Atlantic island closest to what would become the American norm. By the 1550s there were some sixty mills in operation on the island producing over 2,000 tons per annum and some 5,000 to 6,000 plantation slaves, all of whom were Africans."[3]

The search for new places to grow sugarcane played a decisive role in the expansion of European exploration and colonialism in the fifteenth and sixteenth centuries. It is true, of course, that the Iberians (and later the English and Dutch) sought many things from the so-called New World, including precious metals, trade routes, exotic spices, and new land to claim in the names of their monarchs. But, practically speaking, it was pursuit of the "white

3. Herbert Klein, "The Atlantic Slave Trade to 1650" in *Tropical Babylons*, ed. Stuart N. Schwartz (Chapel Hill: University of North Carolina Press, 2004), 204.

gold" of sugar that drove the first phase of European colonial land occupation and development. From the Madeiras to the Canaries to the West Coast of Africa to Brazil and the Caribbean, the Iberians moved from island to island in search of places where sugarcane could flourish. It is undeniable that the pursuit of sugar was a major driver of the expansion of trans-Atlantic trade. It was thus no accident that Columbus, the son-in-law of a wealthy Madeira sugar grower, carried sugarcane plantings with him on his second New World voyage in 1493. By 1516, sugarcane was being harvested, thanks to enslaved African labor, on the Caribbean island of Santo Domingo, the first sugar plantations of the western Atlantic. By 1526, Brazilian plantations were shipping commercial quantities of sugar back to Europe.

As it became more widely available, demand for sugar increased, especially among European elites. The seeming inexhaustibility of demand—much like fossil fuels today—made sugar a very attractive venture for investment, even though the capital needed to found a sugar plantation was substantial (as were the speculative risks of bankruptcy). Sugar plantations were thus something more than agricultural enterprises. From the very beginning they serviced translocal markets in the name of massive (for its time) wealth accumulation. Sugar plantations were the birthplace of industrialized agriculture and an incubator for global capitalism. As Mintz puts it, "the plantation was an absolutely unprecedented social, economic and political institution, and by no means simply an innovation in the organization of agriculture."[4] Historians have described sugar making as the most industrialized form of human activity anywhere in the world in the early modern period.[5] Industry chased the seemingly inexhaustible demand for sweet-

4. Sidney W. Mintz in Ramiro Guerra y Sanchez, *Sugar and Society in the Caribbean* (New Haven: Yale University Press, 1964), xiv.

5. Richard B. Sheridan, "The Plantation Revolution and the Industrial Revolution, 1625–1775," *Caribbean Studies* 9, no. 3 (1969): 5–25.

ness, seeking new sites and methods to expand the production of sugar and to make it more efficient and profitable.

European colonization in the fifteenth and sixteenth centuries was thus a sucropolitical venture. And, to truly appreciate the intensity of early modern sucropolitics one has to understand how much *power* was needed to convert sugarcane into sugar. There were many steps involved in the process: sugarcane had to be planted, weeded, and manured until the stalks reached maturity after about fifteen months. Then, the cane had to be cut by hand and rapidly processed within a day or two. Time was of the essence because the cane soured quickly—this meant a large labor force, roughly 100 workers per plantation. The thick, bamboo-like cuttings had to be crushed in a mill to extract juice. Workers next boiled the juice to purge impurities and to cure and crystallize it, creating molasses, muscavado, and white sugars through varying degrees of clarification. As compared with other kinds of colonial agriculture—tobacco, coffee, indigo, and even cotton—this was hard and dangerous work, especially the cutting and milling phases, where limbs were frequently lost or mangled. Deadly fires were common, as was scalding from boiling liquid.

There were many sources of power on a sugar plantation including animal labor and hydropower, where available. But mass human labor was crucial everywhere and European plantation masters relied almost exclusively upon slaves and bound servants to make sugar because few would work voluntarily in such an arduous and life-threatening environment. In Brazil, the first seventy years or so of sugar making depended upon the enslavement of Indigenous peoples. But as they retreated away from the coastal plantations, the Iberian and later Dutch, British, and French plantation masters shifted wholly to imported African slaves, whom they viewed as a kinless and landless labor force who could not escape their situation. Plantation slaves represented, in this respect, a forerunner of the mobile and expendable industrial labor force desired by modern capitalists. As one foreign observer of a Brazilian *engenho* (sugar mill) described, "they use their slaves very strictly in making them work immeasurably, and the worse they use them, the more useful they find them."[6] Geographer Kathryn Yusoff puts it well: in their colonization of the New World, Europeans violently organized "human property as extractable energy properties."[7]

Among its lesser-known inventions, the sugar plantation may also have birthed the "bullshit job," make-work aimed simply at keeping workers busy, exhausted, and docile. As historian Richard Dunn explains, "The planter needs a large labor force at crop time, but not during the slow six months of the year from July through December. Yet the seventeenth-century slave-owning planter had to keep his laborers fully occupied in the slow months, as well as in crop time, to forestall mischief and rebellion. So he put them to work in the fields with hoes instead of horse-drawn plows . . . Men did the work of animals. Such tasks as planting and cultivating performed on English or North American farms by horse-driven plows and harrows, were carried out in the Indies entirely by hand."[8]

Alongside the constitution of a modern labor force, the *engenhos* stimulated the use of mechanical technology in the conversion of natural resources into wealth. In the early 1600s the ancient, or at best medieval, technology borrowed from the Mediterranean sugar industry saw New World innovations like the vertical three-roller mill that as much as tripled sugar production per worker.[9] Like its Spanish cognate, *ingenio*, the word *engenho* meant both machine and ingenuity. As historian John Crowley writes, Europeans consistently deflected attention away from the predominant role of slavery in sugar making, preferring to conceptualize it instead as

6. Stuart B. Schwartz, "A Commonwealth within Itself," in *Tropical Babylons*, ed. Stuart N. Schwartz (Chapel Hill: University of North Carolina Press, 2004), 176.

7. Kathryn Yusoff, *A Billion Black Anthropocenes or None* (Minneapolis: University of Minnesota Press, 2018), 50.

8. Richard S. Dunn, *Sugar and Slaves* (Chapel Hill: University of North Carolina Press, 1972), 198–200.

9. John Daniels and Christian Daniels, "The Origin of the Sugarcane Roller Mill," *Technology and Culture* 29, no. 3 (1988): 493–535.

one of Europe's great technological achievements: "Sugar fascinated many early modern Europeans because machines made it, and they loved machines."[10] Sugar machinery became a universal spectacle of European technological prowess and superiority.

Sucropolitics thus played its part in solidifying the idea that technology was the leading edge of progress, thereby discounting the contributions of human and animal labor to productivity and profit. As the Dutch and British became involved in sugar making in Brazil and the Caribbean in the seventeenth century, they brought with them artists who produced highly detailed representations of the machine works of *engenhos*. More than just artworks, these were technical illustrations and industrial blueprints, creating portable modes of knowledge that could be utilized by would-be entrepreneurs to expand the plantation complex to new sites.[11]

And spread they did. In the seventeenth and eighteenth centuries, every European country with a navy sought its place on the sugar frontier. Intra-European rivalries, military interventions, and political intrigue spun like cotton candy around the sugar boom. First the Dutch, and later the British and French, featured sugar centrally in their imperial ambitions. Technical and economic innovations multiplied. The Dutch West India Company helped pioneer vertical integration as a capitalist strategy in the mid-seventeenth century, controlling all aspects of sugar making from production to transportation to commercialization.[12] But the expansion of British colonial ventures in the Caribbean was pivotal. As Mintz puts it, "England fought the most, conquered the most colonies, imported the most slaves . . . and went furthest and fastest in creating a plantation system."[13]

10. John E. Crowley, "Sugar Machines: Picturing Industrialized Slavery," *American Historical Review* April 2016: 403–436.

11. See, e.g., Samuel Martin, *An Essay on Plantership* (Antigua: Robert Mearns, 1785).

12. Schwartz, "A Commonwealth within Itself," 166.

13. Mintz, *Sweetness and Power*, 38.

The British colony of Barbados overtook Brazil as the epicenter of sugar production in the latter half of the seventeenth century. English planters joined the vanguard of European scientific, technological, and economic innovation in the seventeenth and eighteenth centuries.[14] An experimental steam engine was designed and put to work in a Jamaican sugar mill in 1768. *This was the first known application of steam power to the operation of machinery in manufacturing.*[15] And it happened almost a decade before the Watt engine was commercialized in Europe. Early "fire engines," as they were then called, replaced mules rather than human labor, but the logic of intensifying production was everywhere consistent. Barbadian plantations were larger and more capital intensive than their Iberian forebears and they pioneered a system of "gang labor with its lockstep discipline and liberal use of the whip to force slaves to work as hard as possible."[16] The systematic violence of field and mill labor extended to every aspect of slave life, which was more often than not filled with hunger, abuse, and torment at the hands of plantation masters and overseers.[17]

The aim of the violence succeeded. Productivity in the British West Indies far outpaced Iberian plantations in a matter of decades, more than doubling exports in the 1660s alone. The price of sugar began to drop as it became more readily available. European per capita sugar consumption more than quadrupled across the eighteenth century, establishing it firmly in the diets of every European social

14. Richard B. Sheridan, *Sugar and Slavery* (Baltimore: Johns Hopkins University Press, 1974).

15. Noel Deerr and Alexander Brooks, "The Early Use of Steam Power in the Cane Sugar Industry," *Transactions of the Newcomen Society* 21(1) 1940: 14.

16. John J. McCusker and Russell R. Menard, "The Sugar Industry in the Seventeenth Century," in *Tropical Babylons*, ed. Stuart N. Schwartz (Chapel Hill: University of North Carolina Press, 2004), 301.

17. See, e.g., Douglas Hall, *In Miserable Slavery* (Kingston: University of the West Indies Press, 1999) and Richard Ligon, *A True and Exact History of the Island of Barbados* (Cambridge: Hackett, 2011).

class. Colonial sucropolitics crested in the late eighteenth century and united political and economic power within the British and French empires. As Mintz explains:

> The English people came to view sugar as essential; supplying them with it became as much a political as an economic obligation. At the same time, the owners of the immense fortunes created by the labor of millions of slaves stolen from Africa, on millions of acres of the New World stolen from Indians—wealth in the form of commodities like sugar, molasses, and rum to be sold to Africans, Indians, colonials and the British working class alike—had become even more solidly attached to the centers of power in English society at large. Many individual merchants, planters, and entrepreneurs lost out, but the long-term economic successes of the new commodity markets at home were never in doubt after the mid-seventeenth century. What sugar meant, from this vantage point, was what all such colonial production, trade and metropolitan consumption came to mean: the growing strength and solidity of the empire and of the classes that dictated its policies.[18]

Mintz argues that Caribbean sugar plantations constituted the first truly modernized societies in the world where people, mobilized through violence and oppression, were "thrust into remarkably industrial settings for their time."[19] The sugar industry also created the economic basis for the European merchant and commercial classes to challenge, gradually, the monolith of the feudal aristocratic order. Many historians have depicted plantations as a curious blend of industrial and agricultural, capitalist, and feudal logics.[20] The contradiction disappears when one considers plantations as homunculi of the industrial-capitalist order that would flourish in the nineteenth century. This argument has been elaborated recently by Haraway, who sees the plantation as a herald of many aspects of modern economic life, from monoculture to exploitative labor and

18. Mintz, *Sweetness and Power*, 157.

19. Cited in David Scott, "Modernity that Predated the Modern: Sidney Mintz's Caribbean," *History Workshop Journal* 58 (Autumn) 2004: 191.

20. See, e.g., Eric Eustace Williams, *Capitalism and Slavery* (Chapel Hill: University of North Carolina Press, 1944).

machinic relations, "The plantation really depends on very intense forms of labor slavery, including also machine labor slavery, a building of machines for exploitation and extraction of earthlings. . . . it is also important to include the forced labor of nonhumans—plants, animals, and microbes—in our thinking."[21] Plantation masters commensurated these various forms of labor through the machinic metaphor of clockwork. Samuel Martin's famous mid-eighteenth century plantation manual was explicit: "Negroes, cattle, mules, and horses are the nerves of a sugar-plantation, for the success of the whole consists chiefly in this, as in a well-constructed machine, upon the energy and right disposition of the main springs, or primary parts."[22] The machine infrastructures of European modernity owed as much if not more to the New World than to the Old.

This is true for the philosophical infrastructures of European modernity too. Sucropolitics fed into the European Enlightenment and modern liberal philosophy in a variety of ways. John Locke's liberalism, for example, preached industry and rationality as the basis of property claims. This equation created a rather convenient philosophical pretext for dispossessing non-Europeans of their lands and resources for failing to develop those lands and resources properly. For all its discourse on the necessity of liberty, European liberal philosophy was aggressively silent on the topic of New World slavery despite its obvious impact on European society from wealth through to diet. Slavery was a moral dilemma, unless one could somehow convince oneself that the slaves were subhuman. The eighteenth-century French liberal philosopher Montesquieu mordantly commented, "It is impossible for us to assume that these people [African slaves] are men, because if we assumed they were men, one would begin to believe that we ourselves were not Christians."[23]

21. https://edgeeffects.net/haraway-tsing-plantationocene/
22. Martin, *An Essay*, 9.
23. Charles de Montesquieu, *The Spirit of the Laws* (Cambridge: Cambridge University Press, 1989), 250.

Yet, as political theorist Susan Buck-Morss writes, there is no way that the European political discussions of freedom and slavery in the eighteenth century were disconnected from "the economic practice of slavery—the systematic, highly sophisticated capitalist enslavement of non-Europeans as a labor force in the colonies—[which] was increasing quantitatively and intensifying qualitatively to the point that by the mid-eighteenth century it came to underwrite the entire economic system of the West, paradoxically facilitating the global spread of the very Enlightenment ideals that were in such fundamental contradiction to it."[24]

These contradictions came to a head in the Haitian Revolution. Saint-Domingue had, by the mid-eighteenth century, exceeded Barbados and every other Caribbean colony in terms of its sugar productivity. Beating the British at their own game of brutal economies of scale, the French colony had more sugar mills (450) and more enslaved Africans (117,000) and was exporting more sugar than the British West Indies combined.[25] The sugar juggernaut grew and grew and, by the 1780s, Saint-Domingue had nearly 800 sugar plantations and 425,000 slaves, exporting nearly 50 percent of all sugar consumed *in the entire world*. Saint-Domingue was considered to be the wealthiest and most productive European colony anywhere, generating an annual tax base of 1 billion livres (about $1.5 billion in today's currency). The wealth of much of the French middle and upper classes depended directly or indirectly upon colonial trade with Saint-Domingue.[26] When news of the French Revolution reached Saint-Domingue in 1789, the wealthy slave colony's days were numbered. In 1791, after much secret planning and networking, an uprising of some 50,000 plantation

24. Susan Buck-Morss, "Hegel and Haiti," *Critical Inquiry* 26 (Summer) 2000: 821.

25. Julius Scott, *The Common Wind* (London: Verso, 2020), 6.

26. James E. McLellan III, *Colonialism and Science* (Chicago: University of Chicago Press, 2010), 63.

slaves and the burning of hundreds of plantations signaled the beginning of the end of colonial sucropolitics.

The Haitian republic took shape with all the might and desire of Europe mustering to reclaim dominion over its wealthiest of territories. Despite its existential precarity, the first Haitian constitution of 1801 not only abolished slavery but any distinction between men "other than those based on virtue and talent."[27] In this, Buck-Morss comments, "the black Jacobins of Saint-Domingue surpassed the metropole in actively realizing the Enlightenment goal of human liberty."[28] The Haitian anthropologist and historian Michel-Rolph Trouillot observes though that the Haitian achievement was ignored by Europeans and their colonists: "The Haitian Revolution was the ultimate test to the universalist pretensions of both the French and the American revolutions. And they both failed."[29] There was no debate in 1791 of the right of Black slaves to achieve self-determination. Quite the contrary, the events of 1791 to 1804 proved "unthinkable" in the framework of contemporary European thought.

As punishment for its audacity, Haiti was subjected by European governments and bankers to what was likely the longest and most intensive campaign of odious debt bondage in human history. That punishment explains how Haiti transformed from the wealthiest colony to the most impoverished country in the western hemisphere. But the depth of Haitian sacrifice fundamentally disrupted the political tolerance for plantation slavery and abolitionist forces on both sides of the Atlantic grew in strength throughout the nineteenth century.

The plantation overlords sensed that the end of their mobile, expendable workforce was coming. Their response was partly defensive; as with fossil fuel overlords today, they sought to delay

27. Saint-Domingue Constitution of 1801, Article 5.
28. Buck-Morss, "Hegel and Haiti," 835.
29. Michel-Rolph Trouillot, *Silencing the Past* (Boston: Beacon Press, 1995), 88.

change for as long as possible through every conceivable rearguard action, including investing heavily in those plantation colonies like Brazil and Cuba where slavery endured the longest (until the 1880s). But they also prepared for a slaveless future by experimenting with technologies that could reduce the human labor power needed for sugar making and other forms of industrialized agriculture. Cuba in particular became highly intensive and innovative in terms of the application of steam-powered technology to sugar production. By the mid-nineteenth century, "one of the largest markets of machinery makers and engineering firms in Europe and the United States was in the Cuban sugar plantations."[30] And technological innovations in the Caribbean—steam evaporation for example—circulated back to Europe and modernized industry there.[31] The nature of sugar making had changed profoundly. It remained a high energy enterprise, but one that was defined increasingly by engineering and technology. The role of human labor changed too, shifting from "being viewed as a metabolic resource alongside the planter's pack animals to an industrial reserve modeled on the power of James Watt's steam engine."[32]

Here is the first inflection point in our fossil hunting. The sucropolitics that had enabled so much of the making of European modernity mutated in the early nineteenth century, both catalyzing and then being absorbed by, a new world of industrial machinery. Much of that machinery was steam-powered and much of that steam was generated by burning coal. I call this new arrangement of fossil energy and machinic powers, "carbopolitics." Carbopolitics inherited much from colonial sucropolitics—not least an emphasis

30. David Pretel and Nadia Fernández de Pinedo, "Technology Transfer and Expert Migration in Nineteenth-Century Cuba," EUI Working Paper MWP 2013/34, 6.

31. José Guadalupe Ortega, "Machines, Modernity, and Sugar: The Greater Caribbean in a Global Context, 1812–50," *Journal of Global History* 9, no. 1 (March 2014): 1–25.

32. Nicholas Fiori, "Plantation Energy: From Slave Labor to Machine Discipline," *American Quarterly* 72, no. 3 (September 2020): 563.

on efficient industrial productivity and relentless growth. But the fossil-machine complex was by no means limited to the production of agricultural commodities. Carbopolitics swelled to involve the industrial production of a dizzying variety of things; indeed, making more and new commodities became its dominant mode of operation. Machines provided the power of mass productivity without the nuisance of having to manage masses of unruly humans who seemed increasingly inclined and able to liberate themselves from master-slave relationships.

It was neither obvious nor inevitable that the age of machines would be dominated by steam power, however. Britain, by far the most advanced industrial economy of its time, opened the nineteenth century with waterwheels established as the primary source of machine energy for industrial manufacture, particularly textile mills. British textiles were already fully interwoven into global trade networks by that point. No cotton grew in Britain itself, but Britain became an industrial epicenter for creating cloth and clothing from cotton grown in its American, Egyptian, and Indian colonies and then exporting those goods to its colonies and elsewhere in Europe. The artisanal spinning and weaving cultures of mid-eighteenth century Britain, expansive though they were, constituted a cottage industry whose limits to productivity inhibited the expansion and intensification of global trade. So, just as they had in seventeenth-century Barbados, the owners of capital and land sought new machines and forms of labor discipline to extract more product out of their resources. The spinning jenny was invented in the 1760s by James Hargreaves, who had to keep the machine secret for some time to avoid being mobbed by angry spinsters rightly foreseeing the jenny's destruction of their way of life. An even more powerful invention was Richard Arkwright's water frame that used a water wheel to spin cotton in a fraction of the time required by the jenny, let alone hand tools. When Arkwright founded his first hydropowered cotton spinning mill at Cromford in 1771, it was quite literally a watershed moment in what we retrospectively call the "industrial revolution." Not only was Cromford the first fully machine-powered mill, but it was also the first to operate continuously, round the clock in two twelve-hour shifts.

Water machines massively impacted the value and organization of labor, eroding the economic basis of cottage textiles in a few decades and creating a new class of industrial workers whose lives would be intimately tangled with the working and management of machines. Later dubbed by Karl Marx "the proletariat," these wage laborers often lived in factory colonies and struggled with the machine world of industrial production, engaging in frequent acts of sabotage and strike to wrest back power from the industrial apparatus and the "greater sense of time-thrift among the improving capitalist employers."[33] The Luddite rebellion from 1811 to 1816 exemplified the uneasy labor-capital relations of the period. Luddites were a group of textile workers who recognized how machines negated their craft skills, allowing artisans to be replaced by less skilled workers. They radicalized and organized; at night they would descend upon factories to destroy equipment and occasionally assault mill owners. Eventually, British soldiers had to be called away from fighting Napoleon to suppress the rebellion, which gives one a sense of its ferocity and depth of popular support.

Waterwheels had advantages over steam engines in that while both involved significant capital outlays for construction, waterwheels ran for free while steam engines needed a constant supply of coal to burn. Plus, waterwheels ran cleanly without the nuisance of smoke. Coal smoke was very familiar to Britons, especially Londoners, who had been burning it to heat homes since the 1560s. Coal smoke contributed to the legendary, deadly smog that enveloped London—the world's first anti-smog treatise (*Fumifugium*) was penned by John Evelyn in 1661 to deplore the atmospheric conditions of the British capitol, "That this Glorious and Antient City . . . should wrap her stately head in Clowds of Smoake and Sulphur, so

33. E. P. Thompson, "Time, Work-Discipline, and Industrial Capitalism," *Past & Present* 38 (December 1967): 78.

full of Stink and Darknesse, I deplore with just Indignation."[34] Yet, watermills had to be built where rivers were most advantageous and these were often in areas far removed from labor supply, necessitating the costly building and maintenance of company colonies. Steam engines, comparatively, could be situated anywhere and when they were positioned near dense urban settlements, they brought labor and capital into a convenient proximity that drove down labor costs dramatically. Moreover, whereas rivers both run dry and flood, "coal was utterly alien to seasons,"[35] allowing capital to disentangle itself from natural limits and variations, guaranteeing productive powers that could match the round-the-clock ethos of productivity that waterwheels had pioneered. Coal thus proved advantageous to capitalism in its flexibility in both time and space.

It was not until the 1830s that steam engines gained the advantage over waterwheels in Britain. But once they did, European industrial capitalism did not look back at hydropower for several decades. The fossil fuel era was truly born. By pairing machine labor with the impressive energy density of coal, carbopolitics created the infrastructure for new scales, speeds, and intensities of productive growth. Plus, they offered a new form of revenue, as fossil fuels are a rent in addition to an energy source. While the sun and wind and water cannot be commodified, with fuel one can both sell the machine itself and then the means to power the machine separately.

The productive bounty of this expanding machine world left no aspect of daily life in the mid-nineteenth century untouched. Ian Barbour writes of a new "democracy of things" suffusing the American standard of living during this period:

> The yardstick of a superior standard of living included not only basic necessities, but increasingly items that made life convenient, comfortable, and "progressive." Items unimagined in 1800, or extremely expensive in 1815, were soon taken for granted as the rightful possessions of a large middle class. Bent pieces of iron were replaced

34. John Evelyn, *Fumifugium* (London: W. Godbid), 1661.
35. Andreas Malm, *Fossil Capital* (London: Verso), 2016.

by safety pins, wax paper was superseded by large cheap panes of window glass. The traditional flint and steel fire starter was replaced by the newfangled safety match. Machinery now turned out cotton textiles, carpeting, shoes, "patent" furniture, and table-ware; wallpaper became the style instead of paint or leather wall covering. To the list must be added cast-iron stoves, spring mattresses, flush toilets, gaslights, silver-plated tableware, and even rollershades for windows. Americans of all classes came to believe they were entitled to these benefits produced by machines run by steam and water, and they wanted more.[36]

A feeling of entitlement to more and better machine-produced commodities has characterized modern northern life ever since. This feeling is closely allied with the idea that massive expenditures of energy are both necessary and desirable to allow the machine world to produce more and improved commodities.

If a single machine could epitomize the revolutionary impact of carbopolitics, it was the locomotive. The first experimental steam-powered locomotives were developed by the Cornish miner and inventor Richard Trevithick in the first decade of the nineteenth century. With attention-grabbing names like "Puffing Devil" and "Catch me if you can," the first generation of "traveling engines," as they were then called, exploded not seldom; and when they functioned, it was mostly for entertainment or publicity purposes. A few years later though, Trevithick's engine would be successfully put to work in the first paddle wheel steamboat. Meanwhile, the first terrestrial locomotive put to industrial work was invented by George Stephenson in 1814 to haul coal at the Killingworth mine in Northeast England. It was named for the fiery Prussian general Blücher who helped defeat Napoleon, ran at only four mph and was scarcely more efficient than using horses. Still, in just a few years, improved designs made traveling engines an increasingly essential technology for collieries. The original purpose of locomotives was

36. Ian Barbour, Harvey Brooks, Sanford Lakoff, and John Opie, "Energy and the Rise of the American Industrial Society," in Ian Barbour et al., *Energy and American Values* (New York: Praeger, 1982), 1–23.

to move coal not people; locomotive engines burned coal to move coal, to burn more coal, in an endless cycle.

Yet, once the carbopolitical infrastructure of rail was laid, it adapted to a thousand other purposes of transport, travel, and trade. More than this, historian Leo Marx emphasizes, the steam-powered "iron horse" had an enormous cultural impact, incarnating public awareness of "modernity." It gave voice to a new "rhetoric of the technological sublime" that distributed powers, previously only accorded to God, to technology's powers of progress in the mastery of nature.[37] Contemporaries waxed eloquent about steam's ability to annihilate space and time, opening the possibility of fast travel to the masses. Some even pondered the moral dilemmas that would arise as steam power gradually relieved humanity of the necessity of physical labor.[38] Could humanity be virtuous without labor? The cult of the mechanical inventor that flourished in the nineteenth century partly addressed this problem by holding forth the idea that mental labor would become the future of human productive activity, an early premonition of late twentieth-century talk of a post-industrial "knowledge economy" and paeans to digital culture and the genius of Silicon Valley.

But the moral problem of work in the era of industrial steam power was a thorny question. Political theorist Cara Daggett argues that coal and its steam machines helped shape a new science, thermodynamics, whose foundational reconceptualization of the universe in terms of energy and entropy challenged the authority of Christian religious doctrine.[39] The scientific roots of thermodynamics stretch back to the seventeenth century and engineering research on how to make the safest and most efficient use of steam pressure began in the eighteenth century. But it was not until the

37. Leo Marx, *A Machine in the Garden* (Oxford: Oxford University Press, 1964), 195.

38. Marx, 199.

39. Cara New Daggett, *The Birth of Energy* (Durham: Duke University Press, 2019).

proliferation of steam-powered machines in the second quarter of the nineteenth century that thermodynamics came into its own as a science of energy systems. "Energy," a term which in its Aristotelian origin meant a sense of dynamic virtue, came to be equated with the capacity for a system's work upon its environment, not unlike a machine engaged in some industrial activity.

It was a sensibility fitting for a time in which coal-powered machines were coming to do a lot of work in the world. But the first law of thermodynamics—the constancy of energy within a closed system less the work done upon its surroundings—was complemented by a second law that held that it was a natural tendency of energy systems to dissipate, a phenomenon known as entropy. Systems were not actually as closed to their environments as an engineer might hope; they needed constant new energy inputs—fuel—to maintain their operation. Daggett explains that the new science of energy offered a cosmological reimagination hitherto restricted to religious doctrine. It was a vision of the universe in which the course of work and progress was challenged by the propensity of decay: "Entropy speaks of limits, of the march of time, and of lost opportunities; it is a reminder that the Sun itself, the fuel for the Earth, will indeed run down. Entropy underlined the promise of technological progress with a certain pessimism, a darker sensibility."[40]

Victorian culture eventually reconciled thermodynamics and religion, energy and entropy, by embracing the fight against entropy as a divine energetic mission for humanity in much the same way that Lockean liberalism understood private property and industry as divine-willed moral goods. "If Earth's energy was running down—a tragic vision—then the planet could not be a reflection of God's perfection, nor a stable backdrop for human dramas. Rather the Earth was a flawed system to be worked upon and improved by humans."[41] Humanity had a job to do, not unlike an engineer's;

40. Daggett, 49.
41. Daggett, 53.

we were to work together with our machines to bring a less entro-pic world into being. Science, industry, and Protestant faith con-verged in cultural support for improving productivity, efficiency, measurement, and standardization, while everywhere opposing leisure and waste. Coal was considered a divine tool and sign of grace that enabled the machinic improvement of the world. The onward advance of industry and the spread of machinic European civilization were necessary to make good use of all the coal in the world. The last quarter of the nineteenth century in particular saw British carbopolitics reorienting itself toward globalization and coal exports, following the spread of steam machines and imperial power across the world, in a process that historian On Barak aptly calls "coalonialism." By 1900, 85 percent of British international trade was in coal.[42]

If sucropolitics achieved its most advanced form in Saint-Domingue then peak carbopolitics arrived in a coalition of steam, steel, and electricity that emerged in the late nineteenth and early twentieth centuries as the "second industrial revolution." The dif-ference between iron and steel is the addition of carbon, but too much carbon and the metal becomes brittle. To find the sweet spot between strength and ductility that gives steel its massive material advantage, the management of carbon and other impurities is neces-sary. This was an expensive undertaking until Henry Bessemer and Robert Mushet developed a process for the mass production of (rel-atively) low-cost steel in the 1850s by speeding up the iron-to-steel conversion time from a day to under twenty minutes. Bessemer's explicit objective was to improve the quality of metal used in guns and artillery. Indeed, Bessemer steel led to a revolution in weapons manufacture that gave the British a decisive military advantage in their imperial expansion in the late nineteenth century. In the United States, Bessemer steel was first used more often for ship

42. On Barak, *Powering Empire* (Berkeley: University of California Press, 2020), 4.

building and railways, and by the 1880s, for the structural beams of skyscrapers. Still, the carbopolitical nexus of coal and steel enabled the rise of new industrial and imperial powers in the United States and Prussia. Industrialists like Andrew Carnegie and Alfred Krupp pioneered the vertical integration of steel industry and the creation of a new wave of company towns reminiscent of the communities tied to British hydropower at the beginning of the nineteenth century. Late carbopolitics saw industrialization and militarization expanding hand in hand, creating a new world order occupied by Euroamerican coal, machines, and steel.

Electricity had a more ambivalent relationship to coal than steel did, but became just as world-shaping over time. Industrial hydroelectric facilities appeared in Europe and the United States a few years before Thomas Edison opened his coal-powered thermoelectric Pearl Street Station in New York City. Although the "war of the currents" between DC and AC power systems has been well documented, a geographic competition between thermoelectrics and hydroelectrics guided the spread of electrical systems across the world. In the United States, for example, over a quarter of electricity supply came from hydropower until the Second World War. In many countries in Latin America, hydropower became, and remains to this day, the dominant mode of electrical supply. Yet, the carbopolitical infrastructures already in place by the time electrification began to spread in the 1880s drew electricity into their web as well, guaranteeing coal a strong stake in electricity generation, a partnership that endures today.

While early electrical systems tended to be local, supplying a community or even just a single factory, the military build-up to the First World War in Europe and North America led to the creation of regionally interconnected power grids to increase the availability and resilience of electricity supply. After the war, those large grids constituted an infrastructural surplus that needed increased demand to function. "The extremely large electric generating stations that were built to fill the pressing and unusual needs for electric power during the World War I survived the war and became, in a sense, a solution in search of a problem."[43] That meant expanding domestic consumption alongside industrial consumption. The price per kilowatt hour of electricity dropped nearly 80 percent between 1900 and 1920 in the United States, meaning that the artificial lighting that had once been restricted to public displays could now spark a domestic revolution in artificial lighting too, replacing gas lamps and allowing access to a widening variety of electric appliances and conveniences in the 1920s and 1930s. Public buildings, particularly theaters, came to be cooled by electrified air conditioning systems. Artificial lighting and air-conditioning together extended the appearance of human control over time and space. Practically speaking, they made it easier to develop the productive powers of humans and machines without regard to environmental conditions. Whole new cities swelled on the basis of carbopolitical cooling systems. And, predictably, bright lights and climatized rooms became new symbols of advancing modernity and its conquest of nature.[44]

The mid-twentieth century saw the second inflection point in our story: the decline of carbopolitics and the rise of petropolitics. As with the previous transition a century beforehand, petropolitics did not simply replace carbopolitics any more than carbopolitics replaced sucropolitics. Each energopolitical regime helps infrastructure the next, and the successor absorbs and extends certain logics of its predecessor, even as it develops its own distinctive qualities and means of world-making. Petro contains within itself active residues of carbo and sucro, just as eukaryotic cells contain within themselves endosymbionts like mitochrondria and chloroplasts, lifeforms that were absorbed by other lifeforms and developed generative roles within them. The analogy is apt, I think, because it is important to recognize petroculture operating at the cellular level of modern life.

43. Thomas Hughes, *Networks of Power* (Baltimore: Johns Hopkins University Press, 1983), 286.

44. David Nye, *American Illuminations* (Cambridge: MIT Press, 2019).

Yet there was no teleology in the passage from carbo to petro in the sense that the expanding dominion of petropolitics coincided with the emergence of a genuine rival in the form of nuclear-powered electricity. Atomic energy was greeted with enormous cultural enthusiasm and imagination in the early 1940s.[45] Yet, after the bombing of Hiroshima and Nagasaki, nuclear power was inevitably intertwined with immense fear as well as promise, especially in the militarized context of the Cold War and its constant threat of nuclear annihilation. Nonetheless, the 1950s and 1960s saw serious efforts to reimagine nuclear energy in terms of safety and reliability, even for household use. Military applications continued to predominate though; and a wave of high-profile nuclear accidents in the 1970s and 1980s, including Three Mile Island and Chernobyl, stirred public opinion against nuclear energy. Although a few countries like France embraced nucleopolitics, its advance was stalled for decades in most, allowing petropolitics to further extend and solidify its hold over modern life.

As with coal, humanity's use of petroleum had humble, ancient origins. As the second most abundant liquid on the planet after water, petroleum was no secret in antiquity. It doubtless came to human attention at first through natural oil seeps and tar balls. Asphalt and bitumen were put to use across the world as adhesives, caulk and mortar, in shipbuilding and architecture. Lighter oils were burned for light and heat, notably in China. A remarkable number of cultures found medicinal benefits in consuming petroleum.

Yet modern petropolitics began to take shape in the late 1850s when the world's first commercial oil wells were dug by James Miller Williams in Ontario and Edwin Drake in Pennsylvania. No one appears to have imagined that oil would supplant coal as the dominant fuel for steam machines. At the time, petroleum was burned in lamps and used for lubricants as a partial replacement, alongside kerosene, for dwindling supplies of whale oil. Things re-

45. John J. O'Neill, "Enter Atomic Power," *Harper's* 181 (June 1940):1–10.

mained much the same for the next forty years, until the Spindletop gusher at Beaumont, Texas in January 1901 and the discovery soon thereafter of massive oil reserves in other salt dome formations in the region. As a Texan energy boom took shape, it became conceivable that oil could be made available in quantities and costs that could lead to its mass consumption as a fuel. Nonetheless, reading newspapers of the early boom era, it is clear how even oil boosters felt saddled with the inevitable continuity of carbopolitics. An executive of a newly founded oil company wrote to the *Houston Daily Post* in March 1901 to express his opinion that, even with the rich Texan finds, the idea that oil could ever supplant coal was "nonsensical": "The ideality of oil as a fuel can not be denied, but the statement that it will finally displace coal to any extent is a mere delusion."[46] The same article advised against trying to shovel oil into a stove, a sign of just how deeply fuel use was defined by expectations and practices associated with coal.

What ultimately turned petropower from fantasy into reality was another carbopolitical invention: the automobile. The automobile has a surprisingly deep and complicated history, one that intertwined with the locomotive for many decades. A rail-less automotive machine was a serious aspiration of inventors no later than the end of the eighteenth century. The locomotive won out for both engineering and infrastructural reasons and was safeguarded by inconvenient legal measures like the British Locomotive Act of 1865 that required that non-rail automobiles travel at a maximum speed of four mph and be preceded by a man waving a red flag. Still, the aspiration of automobility endured; the liberation of fast machinic travel beyond pre-determined routes was a perfect expression of carboliberalism and its thirst for machinic freedoms. A wide variety of experimental automobility technologies evolved in the last decades of the nineteenth century. Many were steam-powered,

46. C. O. Billow, "The Use of Oil for Fuel," *Houston Daily Post,* March 31, 1901, 28.

some burned a variety of kinds of oil; there was even a hydrogen fuel prototype. These early vehicles were slow—the winner of the first city-to-city U.S. automobile race in 1878 won with an average speed of six mph, a human jogging pace. And they frequently broke down. The first internal combustion engines appeared in the 1870s and these often utilized gasoline, which until then had been little more than an unwanted by-product of making kerosene for lamps. In the late 1880s the first functional electric car prototypes arrived and ushered in a lively competition between steam-, electric-, and gasoline-powered vehicles over the next twenty years.

The first U.S. national automobile show—with 160 different models on display—took place in Madison Square Garden in November 1900 just two months before the Spindletop gusher. At the time, most American automobiles were steam-powered and industrialists like Albert Pope believed that electric vehicles offered the safest, most reliable, and cleanest mode of travel. Pope was especially skeptical about the prospects of gasoline vehicles; "you can't get people to sit over an explosion," he said.[47] Yet, by 1917, of the 3.5 million registered automobiles in the United States, less than 2 percent of them were electric. And steam-powered vehicles had all but vanished from American streets. In the intervening years, the combination of Henry Ford's mass production system and technical improvements in gasoline engines made them the cheapest and most powerful automobiles on the market. Still, Ford's wife herself drove an electric car. Electric cars were simpler, safer, and cleaner to operate, but their lead-acid batteries limited them to local use; gasoline cars meanwhile could travel three times faster and five times farther before refilling. Their seemingly limitless capacity for travel was more fitting for a society obsessed with expansion. Plus, with the abundance of Texas crude, gasoline fuel cost a fraction of what it had in 1900. Another sympoietic tangle took shape. Oil helped

47. Nathan Heller, "Was the Automobile Era a Terrible Mistake?" The New Yorker, July 22, 2019.

bring the automobile into the democracy of things; the popularity of automobiles created a growth market for oil that justified further expansion of supply. And so it has gone ever since.

As petroleum became an increasingly essential fossil fuel, new infrastructures of supply and resource frontiers of extraction emerged. Petroleum had certain material advantages over coal. Rather than needing to send humans below ground, often into very dangerous conditions, to acquire fossils and haul them forth as fuel, petroleum seemed eager to reach the surface all on its own. And, even after high pressure geysers subsided, oil could be brought to the surface very effectively using similar kinds of steam-powered pumping technologies to those that hitherto cleared water out of coal mines. By the 1880s, petroleum was harvested mostly by machine labor like pump jacks—in a way, it was even more carbopolitical than coal itself.

Yet oil's lack of reliance upon human labor distinguished it from the dominant carbopolitics of the era. Political theorist Timothy Mitchell describes how the political activity of coal miners helped catalyze and consolidate social democracy in the late nineteenth century. The life-or-death fraternity that developed underground, far away from managers and owners, translated to incredibly strong political alliances above ground that propelled the union movement forward. The material character of coal helped too. Coal was needed everywhere to run steam machines, but it was only mined in certain areas. Locomotives and rail lines moved coal around the world, but in ways that were susceptible to worker's control. Mitchell writes, "Great volumes of energy now flowed along narrow, purpose-built channels. Specialised bodies of workers were concentrated at the end-points and main junctions of these conduits, operating the cutting equipment, lifting machinery, switches, locomotives and other devices that allowed stores of energy to move along them. Their position and concentration gave them opportunities, at certain moments, to forge a new kind of political power."[48] Beginning in the

48. Timothy Mitchell, *Carbon Democracy* (London: Verso, 2011), 19.

1880s, coal workers exercised this power often and often effectively, becoming a militant tip of the spear for what Mitchell describes as "carbon democracy." Where coal workers could establish and defend choke points in critical fuel flows, they were able to exert immense pressure on dominant political and capitalist institutions until they eventually acceded to labor and welfare reforms. The social democratic compromise of the period was an effort to stave off a full-blown turn toward unionist socialism.

This uneasy standoff endured until the Second World War when a massive expansion of global petroleum production for the war effort created the possibility of shifting the energetic basis of the machine world from coal to oil once and for all. Mitchell argues that the Bretton Woods Agreement of 1944 sought to reorganize the global economy on the basis of oil flows and petropolitics after the Second World War, fundamentally linking American (and one might add Soviet) empire to the expansion of the oil industry and the proliferation of petroculture. Mitchell characterizes the post-war understanding of "the economy"—an infinitely expanding field of transactions—as itself a "petroknowledge."[49] It assumed that the world possessed an infinitely cheap and inexhaustible energy resource—oil—capable of fueling the endless expansion of national economies. In this sense, the expectation of constant growth as a bellwether of economic health is equivalently a petroknowledge (although growth is likewise a carboknowledge and a sucroknowledge, as we have seen).

The fantasy of infinite, cheap, consequence-free fuel use in the middle of the twentieth century was short-lived, however. By the 1970s it was challenged by ever more frequent and disastrous oil spills on the one hand and by the disruption of Anglo-American imperial control over the world's oil supply on the other. After the formation of OPEC and the oil shocks, the volatility of oil soared and

49. Timothy Mitchell, "Carbon Democracy," *Economy and Society* 38, no. 3 (2009): 399–432, 417.

petropolitics increasingly militarized on the global stage, drawing the United States and its allies into a forever war to retain control over the energy resources of the Middle East. At the same time, green political movements formed that drew attention to the negative environmental and social externalities of fossil and nuclear energy. A few voices even rose to call for "degrowth" to avoid the ecological overshoot of global industrial civilization.[50]

But petropolitics were so deeply rooted by then that a little pruning here and there did little to disturb the network as a whole. In the 1950s and the 1960s an "American way of life" had taken shape that was, in the words of Stephanie LeMenager, "ultradeep petroleum culture."[51] In stark contrast to the "oil curse" experienced at many sites of petroleum extraction, American petroculture was all about the joys of easy oil: fast cars, economic growth, military power, and, above all, a glittering sprawl of new commodities and opportunities for consumption. Despite the truly profligate relationship to energy that the post-war American way of life encouraged, there was still more oil available than could be combusted in vehicles, no matter how large and heavy and inefficient one made them. Alongside automobility, an industry of petrochemicals developed as a way of avoiding waste and finding new income streams for fossil fuel derivatives. Petrochemicals began to infiltrate all kinds of product streams in the mid-twentieth century ranging from fertilizers and insecticides to household cleaners and beauty products, leaving little in everyday life untouched.[52] Perhaps the most extensive achievement of petrochemicals, though, was its conquest of the domain of plastics.

Where carbopolitics sought strength and ductility, petropolitics enabled plasticity alongside mobility. Petroleum was plastic in two

50. André Gorz, *Ecology as Politics* (Boston: South End Press, 1980).

51. Stephanie LeMenager, *Living Oil* (Oxford: Oxford University Press, 2014), 3.

52. Matthew Huber, *Lifeblood* (Minneapolis: University of Minnesota Press, 2013).

senses: first it combined high energy density with a lighter liquid form, making its routes of movement more flexible and adaptable than with coal. Second, petroleum derivatives were materially polymorphous and able to be reshaped for nearly any imaginable purpose. Petrochemicals created a whole new material substrate for commodities, allowing goods to become cheaper still, more obsolescent, more individualized, and ready to wear and to eat. As petroplastics became widely available in the 1950s, Roland Barthes ebulliently described them as "the stuff of alchemy" and the "very idea of... infinite transformation."[53] I remember the thrill of plastic clearly from my own youth in the 1970s. We frankly didn't have a lot of excess stuff in my family. But when my grandparents handed me a copy of the Sears holiday catalog and told me to choose a few things, I spent days, perhaps even weeks, poring over the colorful images of plastic toys. And what was the antithesis of a beautiful plastic toy at Christmas—the high holiday of American petroculture—other than the lump of coal in the stocking? Coal appeared to possess none of oil's magical shapeshifting properties.

Yet, as one might expect, the history of plastics has layers. The development of plastics started with the use of natural materials that had intrinsic plastic properties, such as shellac, rubber balls, and chewing gum. Then came the chemical modification of natural materials such as rubber, nitrocellulose, collagen, and galalite. Finally, the wide range of completely synthetic materials that we would recognize as modern plastics started to be developed in the nineteenth century. One of the earliest examples was invented by Alexander Parkes in 1855, who named his invention Parkesine (or celluloid), which became an important material for photography and filmmaking. Polyvinyl chloride (PVC) was first polymerized between 1838–1872. A key breakthrough came in 1907, when Belgian-American chemist Leo Baekeland created Bakelite, the

53. Roland Barthes, *Mythologies* (New York: Farrar, Straus and Giroux, 1972), 97.

first synthetic, mass-produced plastic. Baekeland used phenol, an acid derived, as fate would have it, from coal tar. His work opened the floodgates to a torrent of now-familiar petrochemically derived synthetic plastics: polystyrene in 1929, polyester in 1930, polyvinyl-chloride (PVC) and polythene in 1933, nylon in 1935, materials that were considered the height of glamour.

The Second World War drove the industry's growth, as petro-plastics were deployed in everything from military vehicles to radar insulation. But at the end of the war the petrochemical industry faced the same glut that the petroleum industry did. The over-developed petroplastics industry worked to create a mass plastic consumer goods market, with new products such as Tupperware and materials like polyethylene terephthalate (PET)—what makes up your favorite plastic soda bottle—showing how versatile and useful and cheap these new materials could be. Plastics rapidly became a signature material of petroculture just as petroculture became indelibly plastic.

Plasticity, alongside automobility, remains a definitive aspect of petropower. It is also what makes petroculture so difficult to resist. One is no longer only resisting a fossil fuel but instead a fundamental aspect of one's material environment. Sixty percent of fibers circulating in the global economy are now synthetic fibers derived from oil. Here is a list of objects you might have in your possession today that likely contain petroleum derivatives: ballpoint pens, football cleats, upholstery, sweaters, boats, insecticides, bicycle tires, sports car bodies, nail polish, fishing lures, dresses, tires, golf bags, perfumes, cassettes, dishwasher parts, tool boxes, shoe polish, motorcycle helmets, caulking, petroleum jelly, transparent tape, xboxes, faucet washers, antiseptics, clothesline, curtains, food preservatives, basketballs, soap, vitamin capsules, antihistamines, purses, shoes, dashboards, cortisone, deodorant, footballs, putty, dyes, panty hose, refrigerant, percolators, life jackets, rubbing alcohol, linings, skis, tv cabinets, shag rugs, electrician's tape, tool racks, car battery cases, epoxy, paint, mops, slacks, insect repellent, oil filters, umbrellas, yarn, fertilizers, hair coloring, roofing, toilet seats, fishing rods, lipstick, denture adhesive, linoleum, ice cube trays, synthetic rubber, speakers, plastic wood, electric blankets, glycerin, tennis rackets, rubber cement, fishing boots, dice, nylon rope, candles, trash bags, house paint, water pipes, hand lotion, roller skates, surf boards, shampoo, wheels, paint rollers, shower curtains, guitar strings, luggage, aspirin, safety glasses, antifreeze, awnings, eyeglasses, clothes, toothbrushes, ice chests, footballs, combs, dvds, paint brushes, detergents, vaporizers, balloons, sun glasses, tents, heart valves, crayons, parachutes, telephones, enamel, pillows, dishes, cameras, anesthetics, artificial turf, artificial limbs, bandages, dentures, model cars, folding doors, hair curlers, cold cream, movie film, soft contact lenses, drinking cups, fan belts, car enamel, shaving cream, ammonia, refrigerators, golf balls, toothpaste (and thousands more useful things besides). Very little of modern life exists outside of entanglement with petroleum's many forms. "Oil and its outcomes—speed, plastics, and the luxuries of capitalism, to name a few—have lubricated our relationship to one another and the environment for the duration of the twentieth century."[54]

The hunt is over and here we are. We live in a world filled with more fossils than we had ever imagined, forms ancient and recent, mysterious and familiar. We have learned to give them their proper names: sucrofossils, carbofossils, petrofossils. Some of these fossils are relatively inert. Even the once mighty steam-powered locomotive is now little more than a museum curiosity. Many others though—like urban designs that prioritize automobility, the sprawl of single-use plastics, and public faith in the necessity of endless economic growth—belong to a sticky mass that bend the future to the gravity of the past. With this ooze steadily rising, the abundance of the fossil inheritances seems to suffocate any alternative,

54. Sheena Wilson, Imre Szeman, and Adam Carlson, "On Petrocultures: Or, Why We Need to Understand Oil to Understand Everything Else," in *Petrocultures, ed.* Adam Carlson, Imre Szeman, and Sheena Wilson, (Montreal: McGill-Queen's University Press, 2017).

to make genuine change a hopeless aspiration. But, then again, we must remind ourselves that our final forms are not predetermined teleologically. Experimental decomposition and recomposition is more the way of the world than fossil persistence. Even the stickiest ooze permits ways forward.

A quick PSA: The number one rule of surviving quicksand is to avoid panic. Thrashing around is instinctual but it separates solids and liquids and causes you to sink deeper. Instead, the trick of survival is to move very slowly and deliberately in a specific direction. Buoyancy is on your side; with some patience and care, you can actually wiggle your limbs to the surface and begin to swim in slow motion. To escape quicksand is to know your ooze, its properties, its compositions, and reciprocally, to appreciate your agency even in a seemingly hopeless situation. It means finding patience and purpose in the ambient terror. Eventually, you'll realize that small, determined actions work, that the ooze is not as capable of drowning you as you fear.

The second rule is to know in which direction you are slowly, steadily paddling. What's on the horizon past the mire of sucro, carbo, petro? Although other possibilities exist, I would guess that electro is the eventual destination. Robust electropolitical infrastructures already exist and, spurred on by the climate emergency, there has been a distinct and widespread movement toward the fusion of energy and electricity. "Electrify everything" has become a mantra of climate experts the world over.

Yet, by itself, electrical infrastructure cannot disrupt the world made by sucro, carbo, petro. Indeed, if history is any guide, it is more likely that electroculture will emerge deeply shaped by the grooves of petroculture, just as petroculture was heavily influenced by the carboculture and sucroculture that preceded it. We are already seeing many experts demanding more power plants, more grid, and new resource frontiers so that electroculture can meet the needs and exceed the pace of the petrocultural fossils we have inherited.

An electrified petroculture therefore won't suffice. It will take more, and also less, to accomplish the remaking of a world that breaks in fundamental ways with the ecocidal trajectory we have inherited. Retrofitting the infrastructures bequeathed us by petro-culture for non-expansionary, non-extractivist purposes will help. It's better to have a life raft of sorts than to be treading water. But we are also discovering that not every form can be helpfully reimagined and repurposed. Some things will have to decompose. To discern where necessities and opportunities lie, let's get to know our ooze a bit better, this fossil gerontocracy that seeks to hold us in place.

3. Fossil Gerontocracy, or What Sticks Us Where We Are

GERONTOCRACY is another concept with a long history. It arrived in 1828, just as steam-power was winning its struggle for the soul of industrial capitalism. Gerontocracy appeared in a political manifesto authored by James Fazy, a Swiss journalist and political activist of French Huguenot descent. A passionate liberal, Fazy was galled that the revolutionary spirit of France had degenerated during the Bourbon restoration into a "government of old men."[1] By this, he meant specifically those conservative, wealthy, and powerful parliamentarians who defended the debris of the ancien regime. Like other liberals of his era, Fazy was greatly enthused by American federalism and British industrialism and sought a renaissance of francophone democracy in their image. Some two decades later, as the political leader of Geneva, Fazy's wish came true as he helped broker a new federal constitution for Switzerland.

But back in 1828, Fazy's claim to fame was drawing attention to the generational character of political power. One might surmise that Fazy's indictment of gerontocracy amounted to what we call ageism today. But in fact he argued for the value of elder wisdom so long as it was proportional to elders' place in society. Youth,

---

1. J. J. Fazy, *De la gerontocratie ou abus de la sagesse des vieillards dans le gouvernement de la France* (Paris: Delaforest, 1828), 11.

meanwhile, needed a proportional voice too because non-elders provided most of the labor of the nation and thus understood "the real needs of the body social."[2] The true object of Fazy's criticism was the perpetual monopolistic rule of a single generation: "What genius for domination agitated this turbulent generation of 1789! She began by suppressing her fathers, she ends by disinheriting her children."[3]

A more recent example of gerontocracy comes to mind. I started my academic career studying Soviet socialism in eastern Europe. From conception to collapse, most of these socialist states endured for approximately a single human lifespan. The possibility of eastern European state socialism began with the Russian Revolution of 1917 and ended with the dismantling of the Iron Curtain and the Soviet Union between 1988 and 1993. So, it was somehow fitting that when one looked at the political leadership of eastern Europe in the 1980s, one found septuagenarians at every turn: Czechoslovakia's Husák (b. 1913), East Germany's Honecker (b. 1912), Romania's Ceauşescu (b. 1918), and the USSR's Brezhnev (b. 1906), Andropov (b. 1914), and Chernenko (b. 1911), all of whom had come of age in the communist and social-democratic movements of the 1930s and 1940s. This generation had grown up believing in the revolutionary promise of socialism; they had fought fascists before and during WWII and helped build new socialist states from the rubble of war. They embraced state socialism as a bulwark against fascism and the western capitalist states that they suspected were always on the verge of descending into fascism.

In the former German Democratic Republic, where my research focused, younger East Germans often spoke to me about the difference between those for whom the GDR was their life's work—not only the true believers in the communist party-state, but also the dissidents who longed for a better socialism—and those who

2. Fazy, *De la gerontocratie,* 21.
3. Fazy, *De la gerontocratie,* 1.

were simply *hineingeboren* (born into it) and generally felt alienated from the political messages and institutions provided by their elders. This generational split between those invested in the political culture of state socialism and those who increasingly saw it as pointless and oppressive helps explain the curious phenomenon that right up until the moment of its demise, many Eastern Europeans thought that state socialism would endure forever. Yet when the collapse finally came, a great many people also found themselves somehow unsurprised. As my friend Alexei Yurchak describes coming of age in the Soviet Union during the 1980s, "A peculiar paradox became apparent in those years: although the system's collapse had been unimaginable before it began, it appeared unsurprising when it happened."[4]

Yurchak coined his own term to describe what was happening to the political culture of late socialism: hypernormalization. Hypernormalization describes a feedback process through which the norms of political culture—particularly, political communication—recursively intensify. For example, let's say that the political elite decides that elaborate technical descriptions and the heavy use of nouns make for the most authoritative political pronouncements. This was something that actually happened during the last decades of socialism since the political elite felt technical nouns projected a sense of scientific mastery over the world. The problem was that once that norm was established as an end in itself, political actors tried to outdo the norm by filling their political messages with ever more technical-sounding nouns until their statements made very little sense to anyone outside the elite. Yurchak offers further insight into why hypernormalization happened, "The uncoupling of form and meaning in this case was that while these figures were on the verge of dying as biological beings, they functioned as immortal authoritative forms."[5] In other words, as the state-socialist ruling

4. Alexei Yurchak, *Everything Was Forever Until It Was No More* (Princeton, N.J.: Princeton University Press, 2005), 1.

5. Yurchak, 256–57.

class entered its final years—by the early 1980s there was a Soviet Politburo member dying on average once every six months—there was an increasing emphasis on maintaining precise political rituals, on routinizing political language, even to the point of absurdity. It was all part of a rather self-defeating effort to immortalize their political imagination. I say self-defeating because what hypernormalization actually achieved was making political language self-referential, formulaic, and nonsensical to many outside the elite. Fidelity to ideological fossils triumphed over the supposed point of politics: to manage and improve a dynamic social world.

Sounds familiar, no? Contemporary petropolitics has similarly given itself over to endlessly repetitive formulas. Whatever the question, more fossil fuels are the answer. Grid failure in Texas? We should probably become even more reliant on natural gas. War in Ukraine creates a global energy shock? We should be expanding oil production to overcome it. Petropolitics has entered its senescence: regardless of changing circumstances and advancing environmental degradation, it drones on with the same talking points. The petropolitical imagination is paralyzed, completely unable to comprehend a world beyond the glories of its youth. Just like Soviet-style socialism in the 1980s, petroculture today is a gerontocracy hallucinating that the splendor of the mid-twentieth century can be preserved forever. Of course, in the thick of it as we are, it still seems impossible for many to imagine a world after oil. Yet when the oil economy finally collapses, as with the end of Soviet socialism, I suspect the majority of us will simply shrug at how obvious it was that petroculture could never last.

Part of the impasse facing us today is indeed the one that irritated James Fazy so many years ago. The United States Senate is currently the oldest it has ever been, featuring five octogenarians, twenty-one septuagenarians and only one senator under 40. The Boomer generation that suppressed their fathers during the late 1960s now disinherit their children (and grandchildren) in the 2020s. But the age of politicians is not the real story here. Aging may inevitably involve some degree of fossilization as Hegel diagnosed, but let us not forget the wild wise elders, the Noam Chomskys, Ursula LeGuins, and Cornell Wests of the world. They too came of age in the heyday of petroculture. Do we doubt their thirst for radical change?

Although there are many good reasons to bring more young people into politics, fossil gerontocracy is not simply a problem of aging humans. Most younger humans actively reproduce petroculture too. Fossil gerontocracy is ultimately a problem of infrastructure, specifically the persistence of certain kinds of infrastructural fossils, the very ones we excavated in the first part of this book. Some of these fossils are material infrastructures—pumpjacks, highways, pipelines, and refineries—that in their totality represent an enormous capital investment with tremendous inertial force and a desire not to be rendered obsolete. But we also have less material kinds of infrastructure to contend with, like fossilized forms of behavior and thought. True, we suffer under a class of political leaders steeped in antiquated ideas and accustomed to ecocidal habits. But where did their ideas and habits come from? And what makes them still seem reasonable and even desirable to wide swathes of the population? Fossil gerontocracy!

To simplify for narrative purposes, fossil gerontocracy consists of three layers of muddy infrastructure that together constitute the deep and sticky ooze that mires us: *petrostate, petrohabits,* and *petroknowledge.* These layers mutually support one another, and their combined forces vastly exceed the influence of any political figure, political movement, political party, or political generation.

The first infrastructural domain that needs unmaking is the dense murk and muck of *petrostate.* "Petrostate" is a concept that leaked into the world rather spontaneously. Interestingly, no one claims to have to coined the term; after some searching you can trace the first published instance to a passing reference in a 1975 *Forbes* magazine feature.[6] The *Forbes* feature doesn't even offer a definition, as though it were already completely obvious what a petrostate was.

6. *Forbes*, "Be My Guest—But Don't Get Any Fancy Ideas" (April 15, 1975): 80.

At the same time, petrostate enjoys a certain conceptual invisibility. Though the word circulates widely today, it hasn't yet graced the hallowed halls of the Oxford English Dictionary. But a technical definition has coalesced all the same: petrostates are those countries that earn a considerable portion of their revenues from sales of oil and gas. What counts as considerable depends on whom you ask. According to some experts, oil sales need to account for 60 percent or more of GDP, which restricts the petrostate designation to an elite group of large oil producing nations including Venezuela, Saudi Arabia, and Nigeria. For others, the threshold is more like 40 percent, enough to make Russia a petrostate, or even only 10 percent, where Norway gets to join the club.

The same experts argue that nearly all petrostates suffer from having so much wealth derived from a single mineral complex. Petroleum tends to inflate governmental ambitions to the point of delusion. As political scientist Terry Lynn Karl explains,

> "The abrupt flow of petrodollars into national treasuries, combined with decisions to increase government spending, had a profound impact on the state. Oil money was power, if only because it enhanced the financial base of the public sector. In fact, it did much more . . . windfall rents expanded the jurisdiction of the state, which then grew even more as a result of conscious government policy. The public sector's economic role was transformed in the process. In addition to deepening its involvement in a number of traditional activities, the state shifted into new arenas of industrial production, often for the first time . . . [and] almost all exporting states demonstrated a strong bias toward macroprojects in heavy industry."[7]

To cut to the chase of a series of consequences often glossed as "the oil curse," governments binge on massive oil revenues spending profligately, obsessively even, wasting resources in massive prestige industrial projects that frequently fail to improve living standards among their populations. On the contrary, rapid industrial growth tends to overwhelm existing infrastructure, increasing dependency

7. Terry Lynn Karl, *The Paradox of Plenty* (Berkeley: University of California Press, 1997), 26.

upon imports and causing inflation to surge. And this is not even to mention the tendency of petrodollars to fatten the offshore bank accounts of autocrats and oligarchs.

Yet what I mean by "petrostate" is actually more expansive than the conventional usage of the term. Economists tend to see petrostates as deformations of normal national economies. But what if we began with the opposite assumption that there is nothing more normal in politics and economy today than a petrostate condition? Defining petrostates by oil sales misses the many forms of sympoietic tangling between oil and political power that afflict all governments. One aspect of tangle is how energy supplies and prices frequently become flashpoints of political attention and mobilization. As is too often the case, elite resistance to a just and equitable energy transition deploys petropopulism to combat the specter of a Tesla-owning lunatic environmentalist fringe that cares nothing for the jobs and well-being of the working classes. The 2018 yellow vest protests in France against new fuel taxes are a good example. The cynicism of petropopulist elites aside, such protests express the social truth that fossil energy dependency creates an unsettling existential precarity. According to economists, the social demand for energy is inelastic because energy is both necessary for a wide range of daily activities and difficult to substitute. Thus, when energy prices rise dramatically, the entire population feels the rise intimately, and those with the least financial reserves often find themselves in desperate circumstances. There is evidence, for example, that the trigger for the wave of U.S. subprime mortgage defaults that brought about the 2008 global economic crash was a doubling in fuel costs that forced cash-strapped homeowners to choose between keeping gas in their cars and making mortgage payments. Up against the wall, they chose the former because they needed to drive to keep their jobs.[8]

8. Steven Sexton, JunJie Wu, and David Zilberman, "How High Gas Prices Triggered the Housing Crisis: Theory and Empirical Evidence," January 18, 2012, Unpublished paper, Microsoft Word file.

Another pillar of the petrostate complex are corporations whose sole reason for existence relates to the provision of fossil fuels. Upstream, midstream, and downstream oil and gas companies blend tightly into the political structures of the state in any country with an oil industry. Ditto large-scale infrastructural projects related to the management and/or consumption of fossil fuels. Pipeline systems and petrochemical industrial complexes are self-explanatory in this regard. There are less obvious petrostate infrastructures too. Consider, for example, how the built environment of cities incentivizes constant fossil fuel use. Walkable, bikeable density was eschewed in the twentieth century in favor of sprawl that required machines to navigate. At the same time, energy–efficient public transportation was suppressed in favor of inefficient private transportation. Think of how perfectly functional streetcar networks were decommissioned and torn out of the ground in favor of expanded automobility in the United States between the 1920s and the 1950s. Cities were, in effect, redesigned to burn more oil. This dovetailed with the beginning of a global surge in building long-distance highway systems that expanded intercity automobility, challenging rail networks as systems for the movement of goods and people. Infrastructures of automobility became essential petrostate features.

Perhaps the most consequential example of petrostate sympoiesis is the interdependency of petroleum and military power. Sociologist Max Weber famously defined the state as that which "(successfully) claims the monopoly of the legitimate use of physical force within a given territory."[9] Since the early decades of the twentieth century, the exercise of physical force, legitimate and not, has entwined with petroleum in increasingly fundamental ways. During the 1940s, a mutually reinforcing nexus of oil, armament industry, war machines, and state power evolved whose supply chains

9. Max Weber, *Politics As a Vocation* (Philadelphia: Fortress Press, 1965).

and institutional logistics spanned the globe.[10] Strictly speaking, the American and Soviet empires dominated this nexus through their combination in various Cold War hotspots. But this imperial petrostate also clearly exceeded, and continues to exceed, national defense concerns, operating according to its own interests, epitomized by shadowy multinational corporations like Halliburton that provide both upstream oil services and defense contracts across the world. Like the early locomotives that burned coal to haul more coal to burn, the series of U.S. military interventions in the Middle East since the 1990s have burned an enormous amount of oil, chiefly in order to secure more oil to burn. Brown University's Watson Institute recently calculated that U.S. military emissions since the "Global War on Terror" began in 2011 have amounted to 1.2 billion metric tons of greenhouse gases, more than double the annual emissions of all the passenger cars operating in the United States. The U.S. military alone already has a carbon footprint larger than the national economies of Morocco, Peru, and Sweden.[11] Military operations account for 80 percent of the U.S. government's total energy use, the equivalent of 121 million barrels of oil annually.[12]

While it is true that no other nation-state today exercises the global military operations and ambitions of the United States, nearly every government operates a military or security force that depends fundamentally on petroleum for its defensive and offensive operations. And even those countries that do not maintain militaries tend to be pressured into accepting the standardization of fossil fuels, so as to be able to maintain smooth economic relations with their neighbors. Iceland, for example, supports no military and has been

10. Oliver Belcher, Patrick Bigger, Ben Neimark, and Cara Kennelly, "Hidden Carbon Costs of the 'Everywhere War': Logistics, Geopolitical Ecology, and the Carbon Boot-Print of the US Military." *Transactions of the Institute of British Geographers* 45 (2020): 65–80.

11. Belcher et al, 74.

12. Louis Peck, "New Mission for U.S. Military: Breaking its Dependence on Oil," *Yale Environment 360*, December 8, 2010, https://e360.yale.edu/features/new_mission_for_us_military_breaking_its_dependence_on_oil.

remarkably successful in decarbonizing its heating system through a shift to geothermal energy. Yet the gerontocratic-path dependencies of global transportation being what they are, full decarbonization has eluded Iceland. It continues to consume substantial quantities of oil products to sustain automobility and service the aviation and shipping industries that connect Iceland with the rest of the world.

Meanwhile for most countries, the consequences of the sympoiesis of petroleum and military power are that the interests of government and oil industry tend to coalesce outside the domain of political debate. Governance simply assumes that the interests of the oil industry align with the interests of society as a whole. Even now that the intimacy of oil and political power is coming under more scrutiny because of climate change, we find a vigorous defense of the status quo that has led more often to political impasse than to genuine progress on decarbonization in most countries. Sometimes arguments for the necessity of maintaining an oil-based economy focus on national security, sometimes on jobs, sometimes on technological reliability, and sometimes they express the quiet fatalism of inertia. The oil industry possesses not only exceptional wealth but also exceptional political influence. Leaders in the industry know that they enable every aspect of modernity and aren't afraid to warn feckless politicians of the dangers of disturbing a mutually lucrative arrangement. Leaving nothing to chance, the oil industry also engages actively in devious disinformation campaigns and behind-the-scenes lobbying to make sure that any legislation or policy that could potentially harm fossil fuel interests will be stalled, defanged, or, at worst, diluted.

Things are beginning to change, very slowly; the petrostate condition is neither absolute nor invulnerable. But we must recognize petrostate as the deepest and most recalcitrant level of muck, the deadly ooze at the foundation of fossil gerontocracy. Petrostate is the most effective guarantor of petroculture's perpetuation regardless of its ecocidal consequences. It takes dogged attention and deliberate action to escape its suction. For the same reason, petrostate decomposition must be our primary political objective moving forward.

In the intense political resistance to dismantling the petrostate condition, we encounter reinforcements drawn from the second infrastructural layer of fossil gerontocracy, *petrohabits*. This layer is perhaps the most ubiquitous of the three, touching nearly all human life on the planet in some way. Yet it is also less dense and more fluid and thus more directly accommodating of efforts to transform it than petrostate is. By habits, I mean more than repeated individual behaviors. As the French sociologist Pierre Bourdieu argued, habits are always social and political. Habits of thought and action inherit and express specific social environments and specific class positions. Certain tastes in food or art or music, for example, suggest something about where one has come from. A child of doctors develops a certain "feel for the game" of medical professional life through saturation in that social world from a young age. That feel is a social advantage that can later help that child to reproduce their parents' life trajectory; meanwhile, different feels exist for the children of actors or accountants or construction workers. Social advantage is not a perfectly reproductive system. It is more like a probability that acquired habits of action and thought will allow inherited legacies to become future opportunities. Bourdieu felt that habits—or as he put it, "habitus"—are passed on in almost unconscious ways, often naturalized as "just the way things are." Merit judgments express class sentiments. So, if a working-class child doesn't perform well in an academic institution that expects and rewards a different kind of habitus, then that institution will say that the child wasn't very intellectually gifted in the first place (or that they are sadly being held back by their home environment). And in that child's family, it will reciprocally be said that academia is a waste of time anyway, better suited to idiots who don't know how to work with their hands. "Any successful socialization tends to persuade agents to collaborate with their own destiny."[13]

13. Pierre Bourdieu, *Homo Academicus* (Stanford, Calif.: Stanford University Press, 1988), 216.

Petrohabits represent a successful socialization by the dominant petropolitics, a reproduction of the feel for the game of petroculture. As we discovered in the previous section the habitual basis of petroculture is multiple. Yet it reproduces a specific set of orientations crucial for petropolitics: constant motion without purpose, constant consumption without satisfaction, constant energy expenditure without conscience or exhaustion. Mobility, consumption, and expenditure are all undertaken habitually as ends in themselves. Sometimes, of course, petrohabits justify themselves additionally by appeals toward abstract principles like "freedom" or "nation."

Since the fossilization of petroculture is widespread, especially in the global North, it might seem that it would be easier to identify what is *not* a petrohabit than what is. There is some truth to this. Looking at the astounding range of petroplastic artifacts documented in the last section; chances are that your day today will be spent navigating their world. Writing with a plastic pen is a petrohabit of a certain kind. So is eating food that has been trucked in from some other part of the country. So is leaving your air conditioning or heating running full blast while you aren't home.

While many petrohabits are now ubiquitously distributed, the relative impacts of petrohabits vary dramatically according to place and social circumstances. It's hard, for example, to find locations where fossil-fueled automobiles don't exist. But practices of private automobile ownership and usage differ widely across the world. The United States has 200 times as many automobiles per capita as does Bangladesh, for example. Mobility, consumption, and expenditure patterns diverge dramatically in the global South and global North, a phenomenon that a recent research report calls "global carbon inequality."[14] Part of this inequality is reflected in national emissions differentials; most countries in the global South currently have sustainable carbon footprints (e.g., less than 3 to 5 metric tons of

14. Sivan Kartha, Eric Kemp-Benedict, Emily Ghosh, and Anisha Nazareth, *The Carbon Inequality Era* (Stockholm Environmental Institute and Oxfam, September 2020).

carbon dioxide equivalent emissions per capita per year), with many African countries having only a fiftieth the per capita emissions of countries like the United States.

Yet the story involves not only national differences but global class differences as well. In the United States, which unsurprisingly features one of the highest per capita rates of greenhouse gas emissions in the world (21 tons of carbon dioxide equivalent emissions per person per year),[15] there is a stratum of frequent-flying, high-consumption elites that are responsible for *hundreds* of times the per capita emissions of the average U.S. citizen.[16] The richest 10 percent of global citizens were responsible for almost half of human carbon emissions in 2021, compared with only .2 percent emissions stemming from the poorest 10 percent.[17] Only somewhere between 2 and 4 percent of the world's population flew internationally before the pandemic. And just 1 percent of global citizens are responsible for half of the total emissions resulting from commercial aviation.[18] "Affluent individuals can emit several ten thousand times the amount of greenhouse gases attributed to the global poor."[19]

So, while petrohabits may be ubiquitous, they are not all created equal. Through their class culture, a highly wealthy and mobile global elite luxuriates in massive emissions many times greater than even the most energy profligate nations on earth. Compounding the

15. Mike Berners-Lee, *The Carbon Footprint of Everything* (London: Greystone Books, 2022), 11.

16. Stefan Gössling, "Celebrities, Air travel, and Social Norms," *Annals of Tourism Research* 79 (2019).

17. Laura Cozzi, Olivia Chen and Hyeji Kim, "The World's Top 1% of Emitters Produce over 1000 Times More CO2 than the Bottom 1%," International Energy Agency, February 22, 2023, https://www.iea.org /commentaries/the-world-s-top-1-of-emitters-produce-over-1000-times -more-co2-than-the-bottom-1.

18. Stefan Gössling and Andreas Humpe, "The Global Scale, Distribution, and Growth of Aviation: Implications for Climate Change," *Global Environmental Change* 65 (2020).

19. Gössling, 8.

negative consequences of their own activities, the same elite dangles their luxury emissions over the rest of the world's population, encouraging them to follow suit in the name of upward mobility and influence. In a sense this is not a new story. Ever since the era of British "coalonialism," European imperial powers have asserted that the path to development and prosperity be paved in high carbon emissions that bring financial windfalls and energopolitical leverage back to the global North. The situation with oil today is little different; since the mid-twentieth century, the whole world has paid rent in petrodollars in order that an imperious petrostate continues to sustain itself.

Today's global capitalism inherits and reproduces these fossil legacies. It also reproduces the extractivist inequalities of European colonial plantations and resource frontiers. The philosopher André Gorz argued back in the 1970s that the class structure of capitalist society was sustained by a phenomenon he termed the "poverty of affluence." What he meant is that capitalism utilizes scarcity as a means for reproducing social inequality and preserving class hierarchy. New technological achievements and luxuries are enjoyed first only by the elite, which displays them as status symbols to attract the desires of the masses toward them. As the masses gain access to old luxuries, new unattainable luxuries develop to replace them. This treadmill of luxury means that no universal "good life" will ever be enjoyed in a capitalist society.[20] Unfortunately, green capitalism reproduces this trend, emphasizing the invention of new luxury eco-artifacts like $100K Tesla automobiles and solar roof tiles for mansions over investment in low carbon public goods like public transportation networks and public housing projects that would have a much more significant, efficient, and equitable decarbonization impact over time.

Capitalism is not exactly the same thing as petrohabitus, in part because capitalism incorporates sucrohabitus and carbohabitus too.

20. André Gorz, *Ecology as Politics* (Boston: South End Press, 1980).

Yet, for most intents and purposes, capitalist culture and petroculture are functionally equivalent today. Truisms like "it is easier to imagine the end of the world than the end of *xyz*" work equally well for both capitalism and oil, revealing how sympoietically entangled capital and fuel, petroculture and capitalist society have become. It is difficult to imagine a future that is not the ongoing collaboration of capitalist petroculture, which is part of the reason why some feel that the dusk of petroculture augurs the dawn of a post-capitalist world order (or vice versa). Fittingly, Naomi Klein describes this as a war of the world against the self-interest of an ecocidal minority elite: "we have not done the things that are necessary to lower emissions because those things fundamentally conflict with deregulated capitalism, the reigning ideology for the entire period we have been struggling to find a way out of this crisis. We are stuck because the actions that would give us the best chance of averting catastrophe— and would benefit the vast majority—are extremely threatening to an elite minority that has a stranglehold over our economy, our political process, and most of our major media outlets."[21]

The identification of major media as a key epistemic support infrastructure for the reproduction and extension of both petrostate and petrohabits brings us to the third layer of fossil gerontocracy: *petroknowledge*. Petroknowledge is the most fluid layer of muck that ensnarls us. It offers flow and swirls and spectacle; tracking news cycles and events, things are always happening in the domain of petroknowledge. For the most part, of course, petroknowledge affirms the convictions and habits of petroculture. But its strategies are many, including distraction, diversion, and even seeming acceptance of the need for change. Even in the grips of a dominant petroculture, it's not difficult to find media messages maligning petroculture. There is indeed so much very sincere anti-petro messaging out there that if you inhabit certain media

21. Naomi Klein, *This Changes Everything: Capitalism vs. The Climate* (New York: Simon & Schuster, 2014), 16.

echochambers you could be forgiven for thinking that the hold of petroculture is weaker than it actually is.

One can distinguish between a less supple, unconscious dimension of understanding, which is an aspect of petrohabitus, and the domain of fast-moving discourse and conversation to which petroknowledge belongs. To paraphrase Freud, the unconscious indicates the domain of knowledge that is largely invisible to rational attention, yet which at the same time structures many aspects of belief and worldview. This domain, which is also sometimes described as ideology,[22] sets conditions of possibility for knowledge and debate, for example the widespread conviction that economic growth is always good. Bedrock certainties of petrohabitus operate in the shadows of consciousness, so to speak; they are difficult to identify and examine critically and are thus quite consequential for how people engage and interpret the events of their lives. Expressions of petroknowledge, in contrast, may be forceful but they are also more ephemeral. Petroknowledge surges and whirls in reaction to the kaleidoscopic churn of the wider world. Petroknowledge can be straightforward and literal, offering triumphal assertions of the necessity of the petrocultural world order. But, in the deepening shadow of the Anthropocene, petroknowledge is increasingly wily, opting to make its case more circuitously. Contemporary petroknowledge frequently twists logic and revels in misdirection, creating surreal, knotted narratives that often scarcely conceal outright contradictions. Petroknowledge is the original post-truth.

Examples of petroknowledge are literally multitudinous, so let me offer just two cases—one more literal and the other knottier—harvested from the mediascape of my adoptive petropolis, Houston. Houston is an excellent place to encounter petroknowledge, indeed to study fossil gerontocracy in its totality. Houston features the largest conglomeration of fossil fuel and petrochemical infrastructure in the western hemisphere and is home to some 5,000 energy

22. Dominic Boyer, *The Life Informatic* (Ithaca: Cornell University Press, 2013), 173–74.

companies, most of which work diligently to make the insanity of ongoing fossil fuel use seem not only reasonable and widely beneficial but also inevitable. Given this intimacy, Houston exudes petroknowledge with a special vitality. Many key talking points and narrative strategies originate here.

My first example is an opinion piece published several years ago in the *Houston Chronicle,* the local newspaper of record. The author is Kathleen Hartnett-White, a veteran Republican political operative and former member of the Texas Commission on Environmental Quality. The piece lauds the positive, indeed emancipatory, role fossil fuels have played in human history. Here is an excerpt:

> When mankind first accessed fossil fuels, not so historically long ago, human living conditions began dramatic and sustained improvements. First harnessed in the Industrial Revolution a mere 200 years ago, fossil fuels have made modern living standards possible and have released whole populations from backbreaking labor and abject poverty.
>
> Before this game-changing energy revolution, the total energy available for human use was circumscribed by the limited flow of solar energy regularly captured in plants through photosynthesis. Fuel for heat was derived almost entirely from trees and woody plants. Food, clothing, shelter and materials depended on plant growth—and on animals also dependent on plant growth. Natural disasters and political upheaval regularly shrank the energy supplied by living nature. Physical conditions across societies and eras throughout history, of course, differed, but there was no sustained upward trend until the concentrated energy in hydrocarbons—a form of ancient nature—was tapped.[23]

Although Hartnett-White has been lately described as a fringe thinker and conspiracy theorist, her discourse is a completely mainstream and cogent expression of petroknowledge. Even if fossil fuels have an environmental downside—a point which Hartnett-White,

23. Kathleen Hartnett White, "Fossil Fuels Offer Human Benefits that Renewable Energy Sources Can't Match," *Houston Chronicle,* June 21, 2014, https://www.houstonchronicle.com/opinion/outlook/article/Fossil-fuels -offer-human-benefits-that-renewable-5569986.php.

to be clear, also vigorously contests—oil's fundamental contribution to humanity's "sustained upward trend" means that it has been, and will continue to be, on balance a positive force in human history. For petroculture celebrants like Hartnett-White, the category of "humanity" clearly only includes and values the white, northern humans, who indeed have benefited massively from petroculture. Such petroknowledge intertwines today with authoritarian political movements in a way that issues a stark reminder that petrostate has never had any particular affinity for democracy, indeed quite the contrary. As the decorative flesh of petroliberalism rots away, the skeletal petrostate left behind is increasingly naked in its intention to ditch democratic institutions and practices in the name of maintaining a petrocultural world order by fiat.

My second example is more elusive, and better expresses the various Trojan horses that petroknowledge has begun scattering around to advertise itself as being open to change while in fact resisting any significant shift in petropolitics. The example comes courtesy of Bobby Tudor, a highly influential Houston energy financier, civic leader, and philanthropist, who, among other things, played a key role in financing the fracking boom in West Texas. In a January 2020 speech that quickly became legendary among Houston's elite, addressing the Greater Houston Partnership chamber of commerce, Tudor appeared to break ranks with his fellow petrostate agents by arguing that it was time for Houston to commit to decarbonization. Specifically, on a red, white, and blue slide, Tudor laid out "four key thoughts":

1. The Energy Industry has been very, very good to Houston.
2. Oil and Gas production and consumption are not disappearing anytime soon; but . . .
3. The traditional Oil and Gas business is not likely to be the same engine for growth in Houston for the next 25 years, that it's been in the past 25 years. And . . .
4. As Houston business leaders, we have both an opportunity and a responsibility to lead the transition to a cleaner, more efficient and more sustainable, low-carbon world.

That this rather modest intervention caused such local shockwaves says more about the depth and tenacity of Houston's petrostate than it does about Tudor's capacity for a revolutionary vision. Yet Tudor clarified in subsequent interviews that his thoughts were meant as a direct challenge to Houston's "business as usual."[24] He described the idea that Houston had meaningfully diversified its economy beyond oil and gas as a "myth," given that "in greater Houston, in our region, approximately 40 percent of our jobs are either direct or induced energy industry jobs. That's a very, very high percentage by any measure, even if you compare it to entertainment in Los Angeles, or automobiles in Detroit, or finance in New York City."

Subsequent discussion revealed that Tudor's keynote was not intended as a genuine challenge to either petrostate or petrohabits, however. For one thing, by justifying the whole intervention through the need to maintain economic growth, he already signals his desire to stay the petropolitical course. And the pathway that Tudor imagines to a "more sustainable, low-carbon world" is one that is heavily freighted with petrocultural assumptions. When asked, for example, how he imagined Houston ought to participate in sustainable decarbonization he cited "all things carbon-capture-use-and-storage [CCUS] related, and all things hydrogen related." CCUS and hydrogen have lately become standard "alternative energy" talking points within the fossil fuel industry because their imagined futures maintain the relevance of oil and gas expertise, the value of fossil fuel assets, and the integrity of legacy infrastructural systems. Yet, CCUS and hydrogen have thus far proven to be expensive experimental boondoggles that are likely decades away from being able to offer any meaningful assistance to climate action.[25] They

24. See, e.g., https://www.resources.org/resources-radio/houston-we-have-an-opportunity-the-future-of-energy-with-bobby-tudor/.
25. Chemical engineer and hydrogen expert Paul Martin eloquently explains how the current hydrogen hype is a fossil fuel industry delay strategy. "For the fossil fuel industry, hydrogen's the no-lose bet. It's win-win. Either it delays electrification. And by so doing, the oil and gas companies win as a result of that delay, or they get dragged into the future

represent overtures for new public-funded research subsidies more than genuine transition strategies. A decade ago, advanced biofuels played a similarly phantasmatic role for the fossil fuel industry. Oil and gas industry experts and allies present these technologies to the public in a paternalistic way to assure them that legacy energy industries care about a sustainable future. In truth, they are delay tactics, serving as a political pressure release valve to stave off calls for a more rapid and fundamental energy transition of the kind that Tudor himself waves away as being economically "prohibitive."

Then, in the final act comes the reveal. Tudor explains,

> One of the things I worry about is something we've just actually recently experienced, which is that underinvestment in the incumbent oil and gas world can lead to humongous disruptions that I believe ultimately will actually slow progress toward the transition. Because what happens when the consumers of energy face enormous price shocks is they get very, very focused on what they're paying for their energy, and they get unhappy, if you will. And we need a transition that is orderly. We need a transition that continues to supply reliable and affordable energy to the consumers of it, and we need to be producing enough free cash flow that energy players can use it to invest in new parts of the business. And so you roll all that together, and the volatility that we've recently had with prices is, in my mind, actually not helpful to the energy transition.[26]

Yes, you read that correctly. Tudor is arguing that we need more investment in oil and gas to achieve the energy transition. This kind of subterfuge is increasingly the norm for petroknowledge. Recognizing that an environmentally destabilizing world no longer supports narratives of oil-fueled prosperity, petroknowledge resorts to elaborate circuitous and fatalistic reasoning to make the perpetuation of the petro status quo seem reasonable. The kicker, in Tudor's

---

of energy supply in a decarbonized future by virtue of massive amounts of government subsidy for the production of hydrogen, from their fossil assets." https://podcasts.apple.com/us/podcast/the-hc-insider-podcast/id1512721188?i=1000538440409

26. https://www.resources.org/resources-radio/houston-we-have-an-opportunity-the-future-of-energy-with-bobby-tudor/.

case, is that he is by all accounts quite sincere in his belief that he is helping the progress of decarbonization. In this way, he repeats the delusional thinking of the aging generation of Soviet socialists; the world they built is dying, but rather than accept its necessary decomposition they focus on preserving current norms and forms, while spinning fabulist tales of renaissance and redemption.

More than petrohabits and petrostate, petroknowledge is experientially familiar. We see it coming and recognize many of its persuasion tactics as it arrives. But familiarity can be deceptive; petroknowledge has proven itself extremely adept at conjuring reasonableness from lies and half-truths. I like to think of petroknowledge as akin to the watery layer of a clear lake that has a muddy bottom. From a distance everything looks quite transparent and easy to traverse. But the moment you start walking into the lake to appreciate its clarity, the lower layers start to churn up and pretty soon there is a chaos of sediments.

Though I have focused on specific instances of petroknowledge, I fully acknowledge the enabling power of institutional infrastructures of petro-media, petro-education, and so on. Without secure channels and platforms disseminating its messages, petroknowledge would be far less effective than it is. Petroknowledge has many media allies. The advertising industry, for example, creates myriad spectacles of high–emissions commodities and experiences and tethers narratives of happiness and "the good life" to them. Meanwhile, petrostates spare no expense to fill schools and textbooks and educators' heads with the inevitability of petroculture and the existential dangers of its demise. Although the campus fossil fuel divestment movement has achieved some high-profile successes in recent years, only around sixty of the 4,000 colleges and universities in the United States have actually made a divestment pledge (about 1.5 percent).[27] Fewer institutions still have under-

---

27. See, e.g., https://mashable.com/article/how-to-get-university -college-divest-fossil-fuels.

taken an honest and thorough accounting of their entanglement with fossil fuels.

This is by no means to diminish those who utilize media and education to call for the end of petroculture. These acts, however humble, are heroic under today's conditions. They contribute to the wriggling free of the many layers of fossil gerontocracy's muck. Understanding what gerontocracy is and how it operates also helps illuminate the necessity of political change, even under the triply miresome conditions of petrostate, petrohabits, and petro-knowledge. Let's talk more about that change, about the distant shores toward which we are paddling, and what might help us in our journey. Let's talk about the importance of creating revolutionary infrastructure and insurrection against fossils.

4. Revolutionary Infrastructure, or What Is to Be Done

I SAW ENERGY TRANSITION ONCE. That same building where I grew up, the one with the concrete backyard, also had a basement that was a wonderland of technologies from bygone years. There was a wooden high tank toilet for example, a Victorian-era invention that I have literally never seen anywhere else in my life. But the most spectacular relic was the massive steel furnace installed to burn coal to heat the flats above. The furnace coiled in the center of the basement like a dragon. But it never stirred; the building had already converted to natural gas heating by the time my family arrived in 1976. At the time I remember wondering why this dormant monster was still there. I now think in retrospect it's quite possible that it was impossible to remove; its mighty metal carapace was so imposing that the building must have been built around it: quite the metaphor for coal's central place in the making of modernity. Parked in front of the furnace was a steel cart filled with the remains of its last meal, the final load of unburned coal. Nearby a coal shovel was still parked against the wall. My friends and I used to take pieces of coal out of the cart and pretend they were precious jewels. They glittered even in the dusty basement light.

These days I often think about that furnace and its cart of coal. The end of the coal era in my childhood home did not seem to be the kind of orderly energy transition that many of us dream about today. But I also find something encouraging in that when the time came for change it happened suddenly and dramatically. The agents of the ancien regime dropped their shovels and ran for the door as a new world was being born behind them. Something similar happened at the end of European state socialism. In its final days, the gerontocratic order crumbled in upon itself with spectacular speed. The regime was little more than brittle form by that point, a desiccated Potemkin village of socialism. A firm breeze blew its façade over. At the same time, the social movements that had long looked idealistic and weak and irrelevant to the state socialist political status quo emerged from the rubble with the opportunity to set society on a new path. An East German friend of mine once told me that the lesson of living through the fall of the Berlin Wall was not that capitalism was somehow a better system than socialism; the lesson was that all systems eventually collapse. "The advantage is knowing that system change is inevitable. That certainty means that you always have to be alert to what better world should come next."

I look forward to watching the last gas station close and to thinking about my children's children playing in the ruins of petrol pumps. Maybe some future kin will happen upon a barrel of oil in a basement, the last container of fossil fuel, and gaze on it in wonder. I am certain that petroculture is dying; the question is whether what comes next is a better world.

I suggested earlier that electro is very likely to succeed petro. Electro wasn't ready in 1910 to inherit the world that carbo made but the odds are better now. What we are witnessing today is the very early stages of petropolitics being absorbed and mutated into electropolitics. If you read this book some decades from now, say in 2050, this will seem obvious and so the uncertainty that clouds our contemporary horizon may seem very quaint. But the future will have to forgive us our shortsightedness. Since we are floating up to our noses in petro, the horizon still appears very oily.

The question that should concern us right now is what kind of electropolitics is coming. There are electropolitical scenarios that will feel very much like the petrostatus quo, built around centralized militarized states encouraging ecocidal growth in habits of energy and resource use. But there are also variants that will lead toward the discovery of more humble, equitable, and ecologically–attuned modes of modern life. What values will orient electro's world? What legacies will be challenged, what new horizons will appear? Will electro continue sucro's hunger for more and more? Will it maintain carbo's love of machinic work and control? Will it extend petro's thirst for mobility and plasticity? These questions mark the frontlines of social and political struggle today. If we need a slogan, how about: Electrify everything but demand a better electro.

Making a better future is obviously a political problem but I find it helpful to think of it also as an infrastructure problem. Infrastructure is a concept that is fundamentally relational. Infrastructure never makes sense on its own but only in partnership with something else, which infrastructure enables to happen in a specific way. The same material form can play multiple infrastructural roles. The pile of a pier infrastructures a human's ability to walk above water. But for a barnacle, a pier pile is an infrastructure of domesticity, a possible home. Thinking about infrastructural politics allows us to ask, practically speaking, what will enable the making of a better future and for whom? The term "infrastructure" normally conjures associations with large engineering projects like dams and highways and bridges. These are good examples of enablement in that such infrastructure comes into the world incarnating specific social assumptions and values. A highway network incarnates the desirability of automobiles, for example, and also long-distance commerce. It is a massive social investment in enabling certain habits (and people), often at the expense of others. And yet our thinking about infrastructure need not be limited to giant masses of concrete and steel. Humbler infrastructures are just as important and often even more effective. I'll give you a final example drawn from the petropolis par excellence, Houston.

"Houston floods" is a statement of fact one hears all the time in Houston, often with a certain sense of resignation. Truth be told, Houston is a wet place, one that has flooded nearly every year since the first settlers arrived. But this local fatalism about flooding made me wonder all the same. "Flood" denotes water out of place, usually water that exceeded its containment structures and inundated human settlements and transportation corridors. Anuradha Mathur and Dilip da Cunha have argued that the concept of flooding is a symptom of colonial, cartographic power.[1] That is, it is difficult to disentangle the idea of flooding from the historical, often colonial work of controlling wetness, of confining it to certain abstractly–determined river landscapes, thus rendering all other space as "dry" and fit for human ownership and occupation. This is certainly the case with Houston, which has been steered by extractive industries for its entire history. It has internalized the colonial mentality associated with resource frontiers the world over, including beliefs in human technological mastery over nature, in the supremacy of some (white) humans over others, and in labor and commerce as the essence of moral community. Built over coastal prairie, woodlands, and swamplands, Houston's search for dry land has been a constant yet precarious enterprise since the beginning. As local architect Larry Albert writes, efforts to "divide swampland into solid ground and watercourse" have been the central infrastructural struggle of the city's history: "to live, we separate something dry and something wet from the undifferentiated muck."[2]

Climate change heralds more wetness coming to Houston in the short term, through intensified storm fronts and cyclones, and in the long term through sea level rise. Hurricane Harvey of 2017 was a pivotal event in the city's struggle for dry land. At one point during the storm, eighteen inches of water covered 70 percent of the surface area of Harris County, home to more than 4.5 million people. Floodwaters damaged 204,000 homes—75 percent of them outside

1. Anuradha Mathur and Dilip da Cunha, *Soak: Mumbai in an Estuary* (New Delhi: Rupa, 2009).

2. Larry Albert, "Houston Wet." Master's thesis, Rice University, 1997, 144. https://hdl.handle.net/1911/71304.

the official floodplain—while the total property losses from storm damage grew to a staggering $125 billion. After Harvey, billions of dollars were committed to new flood prevention infrastructure projects fashioned of concrete and steel by fossil-fueled machines. It's an open question whether these interventions will be adequate to containing swelling wetness or not, but their results won't be known for decades. What we do know is that past flood prevention infrastructure was both very expensive and clearly inadequate. This is why "Houston floods" is often followed by a sigh. The problem seems intractable in our era of rising, warming seas.

But what if the problem only appears hopeless because Houston is relying on the wrong infrastructure? Why would we think that the same high-energy, command-and-control designs that created the problem—building an extractive industry metropolis in a coastal swamp in a time of anthropogenic climate change—would be capable of solving the problem? I was recently talking to a well-known Houstonian landscape architect, Keiji Asakura, and he offered me a fundamental way of rethinking the problem. Once upon a time, the legendary Harris County public infrastructure czar, Art Storey, told Keiji that if every building in Houston had an adjacent rain catchment or rain garden, the city wouldn't really flood anymore. What is a rain garden? A very humble infrastructure that consists of digging a hole or trench in the ground a few feet deep. Into the dugout you place logs, branches, sticks, leaves, mulch, pretty much anything at hand. And then you fill back in the soil and plant it over, ideally with local coastal prairie vegetation whose root systems can run meters deep and are excellent at sponging up water. As a rain garden ages, the logs and leaves decompose creating new, excellent soil that can be harvested in a periodic process of rain garden renewal. Meanwhile, the rain garden prevents rainwater from becoming runoff by holding it until it can absorb into the soil. This addresses a large part of Houston's problem; the city is covered by too much impermeable concrete while the underlying soil has a lot of dense clay in it, which needs more time to absorb wetness. Flooding, in other words, is a function of one kind of infrastructural ecology. A different infrastructural ecology could adapt to wetness in a more effective way.

All the tools that are needed to make a rain garden are no more than medieval technology: shovels and wheelbarrows and of course people willing to dig and fill and plant. Depending on the size of the project, a rain garden can take as little as a few hours or as much as a few days to create. So, here's a revolutionary idea. What if Houston were to declare a rain garden week and ask its citizens to do nothing other than dig and fill and plant the green areas around their buildings. At the end of the week, Houston's flooding problem would largely be solved, all without channelizing bayous and installing giant storm sewers and digging massive detention ponds and, most importantly, without waiting for decades for a concrete-and-steel engineering solution that will never come.

Rain gardens are a terrific example of what I call "revolutionary infrastructure."[3] Revolutionary infrastructure projects are experiments in creating new relations and enabling alternative trajectories to the petropolitical status quo. Projects of revolutionary infrastructure are diverse, locally-attuned, and typically invisible to conventional infrastructural politics. The radical rain garden plan is invisible to mainstream Houston politics; it has no Bobby Tudors championing its cause, at least not yet. Yet, because it is hard to make something out of nothing, revolutionary infrastructure often captures and redistributes the materials and energies within existing infrastructural ecologies to do its work. The modern shovel co-evolved with the resource–extractive economy of mining, for example. But in a rain garden, those shovels inhabit a new set of relations that Timothy Morton and I have called "subscendence."[4] Subscendence is the inverse of the transcen-

---

3. Dominic Boyer, "Infrastructure, Potential Energy, Revolution," in *The Promise of Infrastructure*, ed. Nikhil Anand, Hannah Appel, and Akhil Gupta (Durham: Duke University Press, 2018), 223–243.

4. Timothy Morton and Dominic Boyer, *Hyposubjects* (London: Open Humanities Press), 2021.

dental attitudes and habits that both created the modern world and brought it to the brink of planetary ruin. Transcendence is essentially a hierarchical control freak relation to the world. It holds that some humans are better than other humans and that all humans are superior to the nonhuman. Maybe the worst thing transcendence does is to try to corset the total excessive marvelous abundance of nonhuman lifedeath into one six letter word: nature. "How's that clown car working out for you?" nonhumanity whispers back at us. The modern shovel was designed as a tool for the mastery of the nonhuman. But in the case of a rain garden, you can feel how those same shovels are now meshing deeply into ecological relations to try to create more stable and sustainable alliances between human and nonhuman forces. Making a better world will take a lot of this subscendent spadework.

But it will also take a lot of nonwork. I always worry that framing environmental struggle in terms of "hard work" (e.g., industry, thrift) quietly smuggles back in the carbopolitics of improvement through labor. Joseph Campana writes of how the centralization of oil capitalism in modern economies infiltrated cultural rhythms, creating an "interlacing of energic and affective cycles constituted by the oscillation between booms and busts" and manifesting in wild swings of exuberance and catastrophe.[5] For Campana, petroculture disposes us to manic behavior even in our efforts to escape petroculture; he instead urges us to resist our most zealous impulses and to explore "powering down," not so much in the sense of turning off lights and turning to bikes but rather by retraining "the susceptible and interlocking circuits of feeling and flesh" to do less.[6] Instead of working harder at being greener, it could be that cultivating an ethos of ethical laziness might well be a more effective tactic for unmaking petroculture.

5. Joseph Campana, "Power Down," in *Veer Ecology: A Companion for Environmental Thinking*, ed. Jeffrey Jerome Cohen and Lowell Duckert (Minneapolis: University of Minnesota Press, 2017), 64–65.

6. Joseph Campana, "Power Down," 65.

In any case, there is no grand codex or twelve-point master plan for revolutionary infrastructure. It has no general typology or theory. No one is in charge of it. Experiments that flourish in one context and set of relations might not fare so well in another. Revolutionary infrastructure is paddling and wriggling and sharing our secrets with one another. I like to say we discover its most advantageous forms as we feel our way forward on non-ecocidal, non-genocidal pathways. It is even possible, believe it or not, to build revolutionary infrastructure within the barren lands of academia![7] Revolutionary infrastructure is like the beachgrass in the Indiana Dunes. It creates a weir for gathering ambient forces and materials and shaping them into new scales and purposes. A massive dune would be nothing without the humble beachgrass enabling its accumulation of sand. Revolutionary infrastructure nurtures and cherishes the subscendent relations that deflate the bloated transcendent attitudes, behaviors, and institutions of the sucro/carbo/petro trajectory.

So, it is high time to ask: What is to be done?

Let's start with what isn't to be done. Let's begin by throwing out the obvious nonsense: the hallucinatory idea of cleansing fossil fuels and the advice to wait quietly for one or another miracle technological salvation. Green capitalism as a whole is paradoxical. It will never be satisfied by sustainability. What we call capitalism is a metastasizing arrangement of production, trade, rent-seeking, and consumption that constantly fights for more resource usage and technological development. Its hunger is sucropolitical, it thirsts

7. Alongside the CENHS energy humanities collective we developed at Rice (2013–2019) and our sibling troublemakers in the Canadian Petrocultures network (https://www.petrocultures.com), I like to shout out the massively inspirational work of the Civic Laboratory for Environmental Action Research (CLEAR) lab at Memorial University (https://civiclaboratory.nl) under founding director Max Liboiron as well as that of the Penn Program in Environmental Humanities (PPEH) under founding director Bethany Wiggin (https://ppeh.sas.upenn.edu). Both CLEAR and PPEH epitomize how academics can subscend their own transcendent inclinations and help model new decolonial, community-focused, and creative norms of environmental research and action.

after the sweet taste of more. Its bones and sinews, especially in the rapidly industrializing world, are still surprisingly carbopolitical, driven by machines and coal toward relentless production of more things. Its epidermis is petropolitical, mobile, plastic, ever-reshaping itself in response to technology, desire, and fashion. You can't reason with this obese Cerberus of sucro/carbo/petrocapitalism. And you can't leash it and try to walk it somewhere to tire itself out. It needs to be starved and shrunken, which may sound cruel, but don't worry; it won't die.

So now that we know where we're not going, we can ask again: What is to be done?

We need to commit ourselves to decomposition, to a *decompositional politics* aimed at unmaking the fossilized forms that suffocate us. Here are some things that can be done with the equivalent of shovels and wheelbarrows, limbs and good will. These are plans anyone can help with, each according to their own skills and capabilities. And there's no great revelation here; if you are engaged with climate action to any degree, this will be a familiar list. Petrostate decomposition, to reiterate, is the primary objective. To this end, join or organize (as needed) direct democratic movements aimed at ending fossil fuels once and for all. Move from passive to active participation in the ending of petroculture. Of course, you should vote, but it would be better if you ran for office. And better still if you were to organize a movement that pressured the political class to change its composition. Outsiders are flooding into politics these days; you ought to be one of them. It's good to support institutions of representative democracy and to demand that they be truly representative and democratic. But it's even more important to march and to picket and to shout and to show strength in the streets. Stand with XR or create your own alliances.

The next great area of decompositional politics is in breaking petrohabits. The good news is that, as just discussed, when it comes to petrohabits less can often be more. The best advice is so simple: re/discover the joy of what is already at hand, care about duration, don't rely on consumption as a protocol for achieving happiness and self-improvement, and be truly present for your relations and your environs. To paraphrase Neshnabé philosopher Kyle Powys Whyte, the settler-colonial civilization that is dying is dying for good reason. It was built on the expropriation of the very many for the benefit of the very few. A frenzy of supposedly transformational activity to stave off settler apocalypticism, as Whyte describes it, only threatens more of the same. The task at hand is the slow, painstaking process of restoring the relations of trust and care among humans, and between humans and nonhumans, out of which a better world can be born.[8] Allies for that process abound. BIPOC environmentalist and feminist activists, movements, and organizations are already leading the struggle to unmake the racial, settler, and patriarchal legacies of sucro/carbo/petroculture.[9] There are affinities, too, between intersectional politics of decomposition and the emergent field of degrowth ethics.[10] The latter's essential insight is that the cause of sustainability is best served by slowing down and being more ecologically and relationally mindful about where one invests one's time and activity. Feminist degrowth thinkers express with great insight and clarity how nurturing the care- or solidarity-based

8. See, e.g., episode 166 of the *Cultures of Energy* podcast featuring Whyte: https://scholarship.rice.edu/handle/1911/112872

9. See, e.g., Robert D. Bullard, *Dumping in Dixie: Race, Class and Environmental Quality,* 3rd ed. (Boulder: Westview, 2000); Dina Gilio-Whitaker, *As Long as Grass Grows: The Indigenous Fight for Environmental Justice, from Colonization to Standing Rock* (Boston: Beacon, 2019); Leah Penniman, *Farming While Black: Soul Fire Farm's Practical Guide to Liberation on the Land* (White River Junction, Vt.: Chelsea Green Publishing, 2018); and The Red Nation, *The Red Deal: Indigenous Action to Save Our Earth* (Common Notions, 2021) among many others, as well as the tireless environmental justice work of organizations like the West Atlanta Watershed Alliance (https://www.wawa-online.org) and t.e.j.a.s. (https://www.tejasbarrios.org).

10. Kate Raworth, *Doughnut Economics: Seven Ways to Think Like a 21st-Century Economist* (New York: Random House, 2018); Jason Hickel, *Less Is More: How Degrowth Will Save the World* (New York: Penguin Random House, 2020); and Giorgos Kallis, *Degrowth* (New York: Columbia University Press, 2018).

economy—an economy that by emphasizing reproductivity over productivity sustains the entire social world, including irresponsible megapredators like Cerberus—can support making a more equitable and stable modernity.[11] My friend Benedikt Erlingsson, the brilliant Icelandic filmmaker, has a lovely way of describing this. "So often when we talk about climate action we talk about the need for sacrifice and hard work. What we don't talk about nearly enough is the amazing world that is coming. You get to work *less*. You get to sleep *more*. You spend more time with your family and friends. You have more fun. When you travel, you stay in a place *longer*. Who doesn't want to live in that world?"

Who indeed! So, trade your petrothrills for what Stacy Alaimo calls "ecodelics."[12] As high carbon consumerism and competitiveness disappears from the center of social life, there will be even more time for enabling each other, for mutual thriving. In a cooperative and care-focused economy, it's remarkably easy to reduce one's resource use to a sustainable level because that is simply what the overwhelming majority of humans have done for the overwhelming majority of human history. Change is hard. Ambient toxicities are many. Unmaking petrohabits, including habits of petroknowledge, can and should be playful. Making new habits should be likewise. In that spirit of decompositional and recompositional play, here's the rules to a game a few of us developed in the lead up to the COP meetings in Glasgow.[13] You probably need a break from reading by now and this is just a lot of fun:

11. See, e.g., Christine Bauhardt, "Degrowth and Ecofeminism: Perspectives for Economic Analysis and Political Engagement" (4th International Conference on Degrowth for Ecological and Sustainability and Social Equity, Leipzig, 2014); Bruna Bianchi, "Ecofeminist Thought and Practice" (3rd International Conference on Degrowth for Ecological and Sustainability and Social Equity, Venice, 2012).

12. Stacy Alaimo, *Exposed: Environmental Politics and Pleasures in Posthuman Times* (Minneapolis: University of Minnesota Press, 2016).

13. Collaborators included Dominic Boyer, Cymene Howe, Graeme MacDonald, Rhys Williams, and the A + E Collective (Finn Arschavir, Ane Lopez, Maria Sledmere, and Lucy Watkins).

Cauliflower Love Bike

CLB is a card game that can be played in a number of different ways. (Get your own deck of CLB cards at https://manifold.umn .edu/projects/no-more-fossils.) We suggest three ways below but feel free to invent your own. The purpose of the game is to create a platform for low-carbon fun by offering you some random prompts to get started. But wait a minute, what is "low-carbon fun"? Low-carbon fun is any pleasurable experience that does not require a lot of fossil fuels to make it happen. A walk in the park or a snowball fight with your friends are examples of low-carbon fun. Flying to a beach vacation in the Caribbean or joyriding in cars are high-carbon fun. The premise of this game is that we don't need to give up fun to reverse global warming. We just need to focus on having more low-carbon fun. And that means using our imaginations and limbs more and our machines less. It's a pretty simply idea you see. And since there's nothing less fun than reading instructions, let's get to the game already.

CLB has four different types of cards.[14] Each type is color-coded. Blue cards are Feeling Cards. Red cards are Action Cards. Yellow cards are Object Cards. And, Green cards are Wild Cards. Each game begins by drawing one card from each stack and placing them in front of your group.

Wait, you're by yourself? No worries. Then you'll be playing CLB v1. Take those four cards and create an activity that fits what the four cards say. This is where your imagination comes in. There really aren't any wrong ways to play the game. The only guidelines are Keep

---

14. We'd encourage you to create your own card lists. But if you would like to use readymades, here are the ones we generated: Feeling Cards = Scared, Lost, Joy, Connection, Desire, Confusion, Weird, Warmth, Surprise, Curious, Hungry, Anxious, Hilarious, Love, Creative, High, Ruined, Talkative, Excited, Free, Stable, Easy, Relaxed, Sheltered, Yearning, Present, Absent, Trashy, Hopeful, Bumpy, Persistent. Action Cards = Bounce, Move, Grow, Lick, Intensify, Hug, Communicate, Retreat, Reveal, Walk, Listen, Give, Eat, Illuminate, Warm, Kiss, Smell, Shout, Whisper, Like, Ignore, Jump, Write, Dance, Laugh, Shape, Shout, Whisper, Wink, Play, Argue. Object Cards = Window, Mammal, Cloud, Fish, Stump, Sail, Fruit, Wheel, Rock, Dust, Bubble, Styrofoam, Shoe, Leaf, Trash, Cake, Bicycle, Roots, String, Grass, Wall, Plastic, Insect, Wood, Mesh, Ball, Tube, Web, Bread, Machine, Book. Wild Cards = Soil, Rain, Secret, Underground, Sunshine, Shadows, Memory, Intimate, Infinite, Cauliflower, Shimmer, Green, Water, Infrastructure, Energy, Weather, Body, Found, Dark, Light, Reuse, Precious, Art, Silver, Wonder, Escape, Becoming, Cardboard, Dream, Emerge, Challenge.

It Low Carbon and Do No Harm (not to yourself and not to anyone else). Here's an example of v1. You just drew:

Blue card: Hungry
Red card: Play
Yellow card: Bicycle
Green card: Silver

Maybe you happen to have a silver-colored bicycle on hand and decide to ride to get a snack near a playground. That sounds like fun! But suppose it's raining or you don't have a bicycle. No worries. Maybe you have some aluminum foil in your recycling bin or some old paperclips lying around. Why don't you make a small bicycle statue out of those instead? And imagine writing a short play in which a food delivery person uses that bicycle to have an adventure. Even playing on your own, CLB will give you a steady stream of quirky ideas for new experiences.

But things are often more fun with friends, we know that. So invite some over! CLB v2 and CLB v3 are versions of the same game that you can play with friends. Divide your friends into roughly equal groups. And do a card draw. This time you got:

Blue card: Excited
Red card: Jump
Yellow card: Roots
Green card: Cardboard

If it's raining outside or you don't have a lot of time, maybe you should play v2, the indoor version. In v2, every group gets 10 minutes to imagine an activity that uses all four cards and then the groups take turns explaining their idea to the others. Group 1 imagines jumping wind-up toy cars with cardboard wings over a big, gnarled tree root. Group 2 thinks it would be fun to jump around a cardboard obstacle course while trying to juggle root vegetables. Group 3 imagines inventing new jump-based dance moves while listening to Roots music with nifty slide moves performed on cardboard. Group 4 is sitting this round out because they are the judges. They get to decide which of the other three proposals sound like the most fun. That group gets awarded points = to the value of the points on their cards. And then there is a new card draw and a new group judges the other three. Play as long as you want and for as many rounds as you like. Pro tip: It doesn't have to be about the points unless you want it to be.

The main difference between v3 and v2 is that in v3 you take more time and actually go out and do the things you are imagining. The gameplay is the same as in v2 until the judges decide the most fun idea of the round. And then everyone from all the groups goes out and tries to do it for a specific length of time, let's say 45 mins. Everyone who pulls it off gets full points. But the people who have the most laughs, maybe they get a +1 for having a good attitude. And, if you do something you've never done before, give yourself +2 for changing your world.

That's it. Pretty easy, no? So put these instruction cards away and start your first draw. Oh, one more thing, if you ever happen to draw the three cards "Cauliflower," "Love," and "Bike" then whomever wins that round obviously wins the whole game.

Good luck and have a great time!

What more is there to say? My final piece of advice is to keep fossil hunting and I hope this book will be of some use to you as a field guide. Each fossil you find is a small blessing. Each fossil you help to dissolve is a gift to the future. Remember that many of these fossils are already very brittle. Soak them with your sweat and tears, keep them warm. This will help to decompose them as quickly as possible so their elements can be recomposed in needed revolutionary projects.

But please don't try to reach the distant shore all at once or on your own. Do what you can; don't blame yourself that there is too much to be done. Accept that change will come too late, because too late is how change always comes. It's OK to be slow and deliberate. Remember your quicksand training. Ignore the petroknowledge that tells you everything is hopeless anyway, so just settle into your front row seat for the coming catastrophe. Save your emotional energy to care for your relations and to help your fellow wrigglers in need. They need kind words and acts. Anxiety is rising because there is so much to fear: the megadroughts, the wildfires, the catastrophic floods, the exhaustion and salination of aquifers, the grid failures, the collapse of food chains, as well as the violent overtures of authoritarian nationalism and ecofascism that resound across the world, beacons for the growing legions of the desperate and miserable. All this is all too real. But, take a breath because fear is a poor compass. Fear is mania, an overinvestment in the now. Mania got us into our present predicaments. So, what the world really *doesn't* need right now is more maniacs. This is only the first chapter of a long adventure, the panic of discovering you are caught in the mire.

Of course, we live in terrifying times. But what we don't appreciate nearly enough is what *epic* times we also live in. It is not every generation that is gifted the necessity of making a new civilization. And that is precisely the task ahead. Like it or not, there is no way to avoid becoming revolutionary. History is coming for you. When you hear about a new flood or fire, the warning siren is also a wakeup call. Instead of despairing at the many sleepers around you, take heart from the fact that even an oil executive back in 1901 couldn't comprehend that the whole world was on the cusp of massive change. Always, we live in ruins, ruins and tangles, ruins and tangles and births. For those who understand the stakes of not changing, our greatest fear is probably the persistence of the fossil status quo. Take another breath and remember that persistent fossils are rare, miraculous even, in the roil of a decomposing, recomposing planet.

This book is called *No More Fossils* and I hope it is clear by now that I just mean no more sucro/carbo/petrofossils. We've had enough of those fossils, thank you! Let the sediments of history bury what we can't use to make a better world. Meanwhile, we can revel in those humble reminders of the multiplicity and tenacity of life that ebb and flow in the surf. And we can look forward to discovering the new life forms, the future fossils we are creating today.

(Continued from page iii)

Forerunners: Ideas First

Aaron Jaffe
Spoiler Alert: A Critical Guide

Don Ihde
Medical Technics

Jonathan Beecher Field
Town Hall Meetings and the Death of Deliberation

Jennifer Gabrys
How to Do Things with Sensors

Naa Oyo A. Kwate
**Burgers in Blackface: Anti-Black
Restaurants Then and Now**

Arne De Boever
Against Aesthetic Exceptionalism

Steve Mentz
Break Up the Anthropocene

John Protevi
Edges of the State

Matthew J. Wolf-Meyer
**Theory for the World to Come: Speculative Fiction and
Apocalyptic Anthropology**

Nicholas Tampio
Learning versus the Common Core

Kathryn Yusoff
A Billion Black Anthropocenes or None

Kenneth J. Saltman
The Swindle of Innovative Educational Finance

Ginger Nolan
The Neocolonialism of the Global Village

Joanna Zylinska
The End of Man: A Feminist Counterapocalypse

Robert Rosenberger
Callous Objects: Designs against the Homeless

William E. Connolly
**Aspirational Fascism: The Struggle for Multifaceted
Democracy under Trumpism**

Dominic Boyer is professor in the Department of Anthropology at Rice University. Most recently, he is the author of *The Life Informatic: Newsmaking in the Digital Era* and *Energopolitics: Wind and Power in the Anthropocene,* coauthor of *Hyposubjects: On Becoming Human,* and coeditor of *Energy Humanities: An Anthology* and *Collaborative Anthropology Today: A Collection of Exceptions.*